WHEN THE BULBUL STOPPED SINGING

Raja Shehadeh is the author of the highly praised memoir, *Strangers in the House*. He is a Palestinian lawyer and writer who lives in Ramallah. He is a founder of the pioneering, non-partisan human rights organisation, Al-Haq, an affiliate of the International Commission of Jurists, and the author of several books about international law, human rights and Middle East.

PRAISE FOR *STRANGERS IN THE HOUSE*

'In a new memoir, Palestinian author Raja Shehadeh explores whether mankind's most primal standoffs – the tension between father and son – against the background of the world's most entractable conflict … The book's father-son arguments reveal the complexity of the Palestinian situation in the Middle East, with nuances that are often lost in the rhetoric of the region's more publicised fanatics.' – *Boston Herald*

'A vivid description of life under occupation, a reality that American readers are seldom exposed to, and charting the surges of politically tinged tensions in his own household, [Shehadeh] powerfully humanizes the Palestinian struggle. Even a right-wing Zionist could not fail to be moved by seeing how displacement, depredation, and deferred dreams play out in this prominent family.' – *Village Voice*

'Raja Shehadeh's *Strangers in the House* is a Palestinian education sentimentale, a vivid, deeply felt account of what it has meant to come to maturity through all the catastrophes that have attended Palestinian life since 1948. At the centre of the book is a classic account of a son growing up in a father's shadow and then having to deal with the trauma of his shocking loss. Shehadeh's voice is a rare one in the turmoil of Palestine: angry yet dispassionate, committed yet free. He is a guide to be followed.' – Michael Ignatieff

WHEN THE BULBUL STOPPED SINGING

A diary of Ramallah under siege

Raja Shehadeh

P
PROFILE BOOKS

Published in Great Britain in 2003 by
PROFILE BOOKS LTD
58A Hatton Garden
London EC1N 8LX
www.profilebooks.co.uk

Typeset in Goudy Old Style by MacGuru
info@macguru.org.uk.
Printed and bound in Great Britain by
Bookmarque Ltd, Croydon, Surrey

A CIP catalogue record for this book is available from
the British Library.

ISBN 1 86197 519 8

PREFACE

This is my third book of diaries. I did not plan it this way, but I have been writing one every decade.

I wrote the first in 1980, a few years after I returned from my legal studies in England and began practising as a lawyer under occupation. I was committed to the practice of *sumoud* (perseverance). I saw the perseverance of the ordinary Palestinian who was determined to remain on his land, despite all attempts by the occupation to make life impossible, as the best antidote for Israeli policies of ridding the land of its Palestinian inhabitants. *Sumoud* was the way I felt I was challenging the occupier. But I was also doing more. I had become involved in human rights work and believed that by documenting and exposing the Israeli military government's violations of human rights I would help bring an end to them. This first book was called *The Third Way*.

Ten years passed before I wrote the second book. I started it just before the Gulf War. There were strong expectations that the Gulf War would bring an end to the status quo that was enabling Israel to pursue its oppressive policies against the Palestinian residents of the occupied territories. There was also a lot of fear. We believed Saddam Hussein might use chemical weapons against Israel, which would mean against us also. But whereas every Israeli was provided with a gas mask to save his or her life in the event of a chemical attack, we had none. Instead we sealed ourselves in one room of the house, plastering all the windows, closing every possible hole and placing wet rags soaked in chlorine underneath the doors, as we had been advised. Fortunately no chemical weapons were dropped on our region. However, many of us, myself included, suffered chlorine poisoning from the fumes of the door rags. I called that book *The Sealed Room*, because I felt the manner in which we, Israelis and Palestinians, had sealed ourselves in closed rooms was symbolic of the way we were leading our lives ordinarily, not only in times of war. We were sealing our hearts and minds and not reaching out to the other. But I was not feeling sentimental. On the contrary, in the book I express rage at the Israeli public, only to end with a call to both sides to leave their sealed rooms and reach out to each other, to meet halfway and make peace.

Just after that book was completed the peace talks between the Israelis and Palestinians began in Madrid and then continued in Washington. I joined the negotiations as legal adviser and put all my capacities at the disposal of the Palestinian team. I believed in peace based on compromise. I lasted for only one year. Then I left, having lost all hope that there were going to be properly conducted negotiations that could possibly lead to a real peace.

When I read the text of the Oslo Accords I felt that years of hard work on the Palestinian legal case had been in vain. The legal, administrative and physical infrastructure of all the Israeli settlements had been left in place. I decided to leave human rights work and for the first time in my life seriously considered leaving Palestine altogether. I decided against this simply because Palestine is home. Difficult as life has always been, it is where I want to live.

For seven years the negotiations between Israel and the Palestinian Authority failed to bring results. Meanwhile, the number of settlers living illegally in the occupied territories had doubled. Negotiations and compromise were acquiring a bad name. The only dignified option left, it began to appear to an increasing number of Palestinians, was to resist the occupation in every possible way. The impoverishment of the working people, the absence of hope, exacerbated by the continuation of the building of settlements, and the failure of the Accords to deal with the basic issues led to an explosion. On 28 September 2000 a second, more violent Intifada broke out.

Unlike the first Intifada, which was a popular, mainly non-violent uprising, this was an armed rebellion punctuated by horrific bombings among the civilian population in Israel. The worst of these took place on 27 March 2002, when a Palestinian attacker exploded himself in the dining room of a hotel in Netanya during a meal to celebrate the Jewish festival of Passover, killing twenty-nine people and injuring 140. It was this incident that provided Israel with the excuse to begin its invasion of the West Bank. The Israeli army was militarily and, thanks to the horror of this and other bombings, as well as their exploitation by the Israeli right, psychologically prepared.

The invasion of Ramallah described in this book began on 29 March 2002. From the outset I was aware how differently I felt from other times of crisis. In the past I rose to the occasion. I saw meaning in my suffering. I was part of the struggle and expected and accepted the enemy's response. This time, when this second Intifada began, I tried to ignore it. Then I became depressed. I had seen how badly our leadership had managed earlier struggles. I had no faith that the same leadership would manage this round any differently. The indiscriminate killing of civilians in

Israel exacted a high moral and political cost. I could not discern a clear strategy on the part of the Palestinians. I was especially worried by the excessive militarization that was taking place all around me. I could see how it deprived the populace of their role and gave Israel the justification to practise ever more brutal policies. I could not understand the wisdom of engaging in a military confrontation with the fourth most powerful army in the world when we didn't even have an army of our own. Our strength was in the justice and morality of our case and we were jeopardizing these by our outrageous actions.

Over the last nine years I have been uninvolved in public life. I was concentrating on my legal practice and writing. I never thought I would ever write another book based on my diaries. I wanted to draw on my imagination for material, not record the difficult ordeals of my daily life. Still, I decided to edit my diaries of the invasion into a book. The experience you will read about here is not that of a hero who took risks. It is that of a Palestinian who has always wanted to be able to continue to live his life as an ordinary citizen in Palestine.

The events described here represent the epitome of a tragedy that has long been unfolding. I have not decided to publish these diaries merely to paint a bleak picture or to gain the reader's sympathy for the victimization the Palestinians experienced. Those well-wishers who called me as the shelling was going on to commiserate, I tried to silence. No one is helped by being reduced to the status of victim. Palestinians don't need to be pitied or viewed as unfortunates who deserve assistance and relief. They need people to understand their cause and work with them to bring justice and peace to their war-battered land.

28 March

I felt the tension the moment I entered my law office. I asked about the two assistants from Jerusalem and was told they were unable to cross the checkpoint at Kalandia. They had phoned, alarmed at reports that all foreigners were being evacuated from Ramallah in anticipation of an Israeli invasion. The presence of foreigners in the town had always seemed a protection for the Palestinian community from Israeli excesses. The news that they were being evacuated made us feel that some atrocity was being planned for which the Israeli army wanted no witnesses. For a long time Palestinians had been demanding an international protection force. I would have felt immensely more secure if one had been dispatched.

It was only two weeks ago that the army had withdrawn from Ramallah after an occupation of three days. They were now stationed on the outskirts of the town, which was under siege. There were two points of view at the office. The first was that the attack was imminent; the second that Arafat has signed the document which General Anthony Zinni, the US envoy, wanted him to sign, therefore there was not going to be an attack. My own sense was that something was going to happen. I felt overwhelmed by a strong sense of foreboding.

One of our secretaries asked to leave early to do some shopping. I too decided to take the precaution of shopping, stocking up on things and getting prepared for a long curfew. I didn't want to be caught off guard. I left the office and went out to the street. Our law office is in the centre of town on its main commercial artery, Main Street. I didn't drive. I walked. The town was in its usually chaotic state, with posters plastered on many walls with pictures of the latest Palestinian bombers. But something was different today. It was as though the place had been struck by a storm. There was a rush on the market. Everyone was moving quickly and people were emerging from shops with heavy bags. Prices had risen appreciably. A sense of an impending catastrophe loomed in the air. At the vegetable shop a frantic middle-aged woman with ruffled hair was loading vegetables into her shopping bag. I saw that she was taking a large number of golden onions. When she bent down to pick them from the lower rack, I noticed that their yellowish translucent skin was the colour of her hair. She looked up at me, 'Onions go a long way. They're good to have,' she said, and helped herself to more. Vegetables from her overfilled bags were falling on the narrow paths between the stalls. She stooped down to collect them. She was creating panic in the crowded shop. I carried my vegetables and left, passing by the Manara, the recently renovated roundabout at the centre of downtown. I looked at the plastic lions, an addition from the Oslo years, and remembered the picture I saw in the daily paper a few weeks ago of the Palestinian fighters crouching behind one of them, shooting at the Israeli soldiers. One cub had lost its tail in the fusillade.

Dominating the square was a large banner the width of the street with a picture of Arafat, his *kuffieh* piled up like a small pyramid over his head, raising his finger like a teacher, his eyes open wide. The words he was preaching were sprawled in large script:

All it takes is to will it. You are the knight of this hour.

Further up the street, by the florist where a gun battle had blown away the cornerstones of the old building, I noticed fresh plastering between the restored stones. The glass of the travel agent across the street had also been replaced. The son had recently renovated his father's office and, rather than install full metal shutters like the rest of his neighbours, he wanted to distinguish his agency by using the daintier metal grille. It cost him the entire glass front. Nearby was the blackened butcher's shop which had been firebombed and its proprietor killed in a criminal feud involving armed groups from a nearby refugee camp. Disputes of this sort used to be settled by the court. Now, with the predominance of arms, people were taking the law in their own hands.

These shops around the centre of town are not far from Arafat's headquarters. During the last Israeli incursion into Ramallah the army had stayed away from this area. It became a refuge for the Palestinian fighters resisting the occupation of Ramallah. All other parts of the city were occupied, with Israeli tanks crowding the narrow streets. We could not move out of our house for three days as gun battles raged. This episode had ended with an Israeli withdrawal and the feeling that our side had won and had driven back the mighty Israeli army.

No wonder the large contingent of armed men in uniform and civilian clothes seemed to carry their arms with pride. They finally had the opportunity to use them to defend the town. A columnist in the local daily newspaper called this second Intifada the Palestinian War of Independence.

✳ ✳ ✳

Just after I got back to the office with my heavy shopping bags, two armed Palestinian security men came in. They said that they had been evacuated from their residences at the headquarters in anticipation of Israeli air strikes. Their commanders had made no alternative arrangements for them. They were on their own and had to find a place to spend the night.

'Had the weather been warmer,' one of them said, 'we wouldn't have minded sleeping out. We are soldiers. We put our blanket anywhere and sleep out in the open. We don't care. But it's stormy and rainy. We need to find a place. Do you know of any empty apartments?'

We didn't. My partner suggested that perhaps they would stand a better chance in the villages around Ramallah.

'Yes, we know there are more possibilities there,' said one of them, 'but we have Gaza identity cards, we cannot get out of Ramallah. It's too dangerous. If the Israelis find us outside Ramallah, we'll get deported back to Gaza.'

One did all the talking. He had dark skin, a round face, amiable with kind eyes. He was jaunty and seemed to take his predicament lightly. His friend was quiet. Contemplative. He let his companion do the talking as he stood awkwardly in our office, wearing his fatigues, with his large gun propped heavily by his side, his eyes roaming around our shelves full of books and paper. What could he have been thinking? I looked at their shoes. Neither was wearing boots, as soldiers do. They had on ordinary black leather shoes. The more garrulous had worn ones; the quieter had a newer pair. Both were dusty. I wondered how they were going to cater for their personal needs. Alongside the orderly, ordinary life I lead in my hometown of Ramallah is a population of transient people who wear army uniforms when we don't yet have an army and who camp out in the hills when the weather permits or in empty apartment blocks if they can find them.

The two of them were very polite and, when they realized we could not help, they apologized for barging in like this. They carried their guns and walked out wearing the emblem of their doom that, in the event of an Israeli invasion, would bring death and destruction to them and to any place of refuge they might find.

* * *

Over the past nine years, since the Oslo Accords, I have been worried about the growing number of armed civilians I could see around just walking in the street. This was not part of a policy of armed struggle. It was more for exhibitionist purposes. Parades were conducted with masked men bearing arms, as if in a masquerade. An arms culture develops as quickly as a drug culture. Once it takes root, it is difficult to eradicate. It has its own economic logic and beneficiaries. Its victims are the civilian society who have to endure its violent consequences. During the first twenty-five years of occupation, before the return of the PLO, the armed struggle had been waged outside. Now it had moved inside. Increasingly I have been seeing armed men in all sorts of gear. This morning when I left the house I saw six Palestinian soldiers outside my door waiting as two others changed the flat tyre of their army van. It is not always clear which unit they belong to and how they are related to other units. For a long

5

time a number of soldiers had been living in a makeshift camp behind the UNRWA[†] community college not far from my house, bivouacked on the highest hill to guard the town from attacks by Israel from the north. I felt for them as they endured the cold of the Ramallah winter. During the last Israeli incursion one of them was shot dead. Since then they seem to have abandoned that post.

Before the Oslo Accords in 1993, only Israeli soldiers carried arms. The Interim Agreement between Israel and the PLO allowed for a strong, armed Palestinian police. The Israeli government was happy for this force to police dissidents and curb civil rights but claimed that it was in excess of the numbers agreed upon.

✳ ✳ ✳

Just after the Accords were signed, we employed at the office a bright young man to do the cleaning. He was overqualified but had lost his job in Israel due to the closure of the West Bank. One day I came back to find that he had broken an antique ceramic vase that I had on the shelf behind my desk. I was angry and explained the archaeological significance of this piece of pottery from the Middle Bronze Age. He listened quietly. The next day I found the pot back on my shelf. I was astounded. I looked and found that he had collected the pieces, taken them home and glued them perfectly together. I was impressed and tried to learn more about this talented man. He was reluctant to speak. In the course of our conversation, I

---

† United Nations Relief and Works Agency

tried to find out what he thought about the peace that the PLO had signed with Israel. I assumed that he, like most young men, belonged to one or the other factions of the organization. I was wrong. He belonged to another clandestine struggle, committed to principles that were foreign to me. This was the first intimation of what the Oslo Accords would bring: the polarization of Palestinian society. Throughout the first Intifada I had felt such oneness with everyone. We were all working together for a common cause, the end of the Israeli occupation. It mattered little that one was the employer and one the employee. There was a strong sense of solidarity among us. Before the Israeli oppressor we were all equal. Together we participated in the struggle of ridding our country from occupation. Now the false peace of Oslo had divided us, made some believe they could pursue their private life despite the continuation of the occupation while others suffered in the worsening economic conditions. The false peace had shattered us like the pieces of that old pot.

✳ ✳ ✳

Yesterday I paid a condolence visit to a man who used to work at my office for whom I have a strong fondness. His twenty-five-year-old son, Ahmad, died in the last Israeli incursion into Ramallah. The son had been doing well as an insurance clerk. He was married with children. When he was only fourteen I defended him in the military court, where he was being charged for protesting against the occupation. Because he was a minor, the court imposed a fine on his father. As I was walking out of the court with the father, I heard shouts from the narrow

7

window above the door where the son was being temporarily held.

'I warn you,' he called at his father, 'don't pay the fine. You hear me. I don't want you to pay money to these Zionist occupiers.'

The military court and prison were in an ugly square cement building that was a legacy of the British mandate. It had been built in 1936 and called after its designer, an Irishman by the name of Tegart. Arafat has his headquarters in the same compound, which has been expanded and surrounded by high walls. It is now referred to as the Muqata.

Ahmad's family had lived in a refugee camp. They had lost their home in 1948. The father did not want his children to get involved in politics, so he moved them out of the camp. But Ahmad had grown up with anger and, when the chance came to acquire a gun and fight the occupation army, he took it.

When we arrived we found that the father was at the mosque praying, even though it was not a Friday. Throughout the twenty-five years he had worked at my office he never prayed. As we waited we asked the mother what had happened. Her answer sounded as though she was reading from a prepared text, delivered dutifully but without conviction. The loss of her son was obviously the real thing, not his heroism, which she recounted to anyone who asked.

'Ahmad was first shot in the leg,' she said, keeping her palm over her cheek, 'but he wanted to go on fighting. Then he got the bullet that made him a martyr.'

I was later told that the real story was that after her son's first injury the ambulance came to take him to hospital. But they would not allow him to take his gun. He refused to abandon it and was shot again. This time the Israeli sniper got him in the stomach and he died. I had no doubt about his integrity. I only wondered who gave him the gun, and under what conditions. What would it have meant if he had left it behind? The only thing I was sure of was that this gun must have meant so much to him that he was willing to risk his life for it.

The father, now with a full beard, seemed resigned to the loss of his son. As I sat in Abu Ahmad's guest room, which was decorated with the usual symbols of Palestinian pride – large uncomfortable sofas, Palestinian flags and a miniature Dome of the Rock in mother-of-pearl – I tried to think what it must be like for a father who was my age suddenly to find his son, who is not a soldier, killed in the course of fighting a regular army. This is the son who was his best security for old age in a stateless society where one's only security was in one's children. The successful working son, his pride and joy, who was married and had brought him grandchildren. How could he deal with his death? He didn't want to speak about it. We spoke instead about the general situation.

In the course of the visit he turned to me and said, 'Do you remember what my opinion was about Oslo? Wasn't I against it from the first moment? Did I not tell you it would not bring us peace? Didn't I? We shall never see peace in this country.'

Between the silences our eyes rested on the poster of Ahmad that took up half the wall of the guest room in which we sat. The poster was a gift from the son's Fatah unit, in appreciation and memoriam.

* * *

9

Having been denied arms for so long, young Palestinians seek them and carry them with manifest pride. Today, as I was walking to my office, I saw a young man in civilian clothes with a gun strapped around his shoulder. He was a lean, tall young man, quite dapper, almost a dandy. He wore tight black trousers and shoes without a speck of dust. He had a flat stomach. His belt was black with a silver square buckle. He wore a knitted polo-neck sweater. It too was black. He was adjusting the strap (also black) of his gun, which was resting on his back. He was trying to get it exactly diagonal along his chest, as though he was grooming himself for a date with his girlfriend. He must have seen Israeli soldiers with their guns and was emulating them.

I turned to look and my eyes met those of one of the shop-keepers, who said, 'The man has no idea what effect this has on foreigners coming to Ramallah. It will just confirm to them what they hear about us and make them decide to stay away.' This merchant was thinking only of the commercial impact militarization has on his business.

For weeks a reconnaissance helicopter had been literally parked in different parts of the sky above Ramallah, photographing. It was an ominous sight; its drone a nerve wrecker. The Oslo Accords had created a three-tiered jurisdiction, giving Israel rights over the sub-soil and the air and leaving the Palestinians in control only of the surface. The Israeli army must already have full aerial photographs of every section of the town.

* * *

Just as I was turning the corner to walk up to my office after I had finished shopping I met Dr Mustafa Bargouti, a popular politician and founder of the largest non-governmental organization involved in medical services. He did not believe the Israelis were going to attack tomorrow. He told me that 400 foreigners from various European countries were flying in to be with the Palestinian people for protection and solidarity. Ninety of them were already in Jerusalem. I wondered whether they would be able to make it to Ramallah since the checkpoint at Kalandia was closed.

✳ ✳ ✳

We decided to close the office early today. I couldn't wait to get home. On the way I felt relieved that I had filled up the fuel tank for heating and hot water. I loaded my shopping into my car and drove away from the centre of town. I parked the car in the garage, closed the outside gate, carried the bags into the kitchen and pressed the switch for the garage door. But when I heard it click closed, I felt something was wrong. I'm not ready for the worst to happen tomorrow. Not with my wife, Penny, still away.

29 March

I woke up this morning, heard the screeching of Israeli tanks scrapping the road past my house as they drove down into town and knew that the strike that Prime Minister Sharon had warned would make us weep had begun. As the tanks moved beyond my house I felt captured behind enemy lines. With my house in the occupied zone, Penny would not be able to get back. I felt as though a calamity had befallen me. A low black cloud was descending, darkening my world. This was not the first time I had been under Israeli occupation, I was for most of my life, but this time I was caught unprepared, just three days short. When Penny was trying to decide whether to go to Cairo for her conference, we thought no Israeli attack could possibly begin as long as the US envoy, Anthony Zinni, was in the area. We had miscalculated. Now she was stranded outside and I was here alone, captured. I knew she would eventually be able to come back, I was sure of it, but how could I not help worrying after knowing of so many Palestinians who suffered for years trying to obtain permission from the Israeli authorities for the reunification of their families. Whatever was coming, I would have to endure it alone.

As I was trying to manage my feelings of insecurity and fretfulness, Samer, my younger brother, called. He was whispering.

'Why are you whispering?' I asked.

'Israeli soldiers are in my house,' he said.

He told me that he was forbidden to use his telephone. He described what had happened in low, halting whispers, placing his mobile phone close to his mouth. He said, 'Israeli soldiers came early in the morning, broke the kitchen window and occupied the whole building. They forced the neighbours down to my house and locked us in three rooms.'

I asked him whether they had an order for impounding the building.

'No,' he said. 'Nothing of the sort. They forced us at gunpoint to obey their orders. I'll give you more details later. I don't want them to know I'm talking to you. Can you do something to help me?'

After I put down the telephone, I felt distressed the more I thought of my brother and his family, Tala, his four-year-old daughter, and Aziz, his six-year-old son, subjected to the brutality of an occupying army. I had to do something to help them. I racked my brains. What could I do?

When I began to review the options, I realized how I had severed my ties with the establishment, Israeli, Palestinian and American. I used to know people in authority when I was active in human rights. I knew who to call, what to do, how to raise a storm, how to apply pressure, to use the media to make a case. Now I knew no one whom I could call on. My brother's only advantage, I thought, was that he holds a US passport. Perhaps the US consulate in Jerusalem could help. But then again I knew no one there. It was fortunate that a well-connected friend called from the States to inquire about me after he heard of the occupation of Ramallah. I sought his advice. He gave me the name and number of the US consul general and another number for an assistant. He said he knew the consul general well and would speak to him about Samer.

I called the emergency officer first, because I could not get hold of the consul general. A woman answered. I told her of my brother's situation. I said that the army had stormed his house without an order. Perhaps the consulate could use this fact to intervene.

'No,' she said. 'It doesn't matter that they had no order. It doesn't matter at all. The order comes later.'

'I am a lawyer,' I said. 'I know that orders cannot be made after the fact.'

This angered the woman, who accused me of confusing reality with politics. 'We can do nothing,' the American official finally insisted.

I should have known better. Before Israel, the US is impotent. We were on our own.

That cursed dark cloud that had hung over me since last night was descending further and further, allowing no light through, leaving me no room to breathe. I felt that I could do nothing. Couldn't concentrate. My thoughts were constantly with my brother and his family.

Samer was so proud of his recently built house. After several difficult years, he had just finished paying his loans. This morning he woke up in his comfortable bed to the sound of commotion in his house. In the dark of night, Israeli soldiers had driven up in their tanks, smashed the outside gate, driven up the yard where his children play, walked up the kitchen stairs, broken the glass of the window and opened the kitchen door. By any civilized standards, these members of Israel Defence Forces were burglars, for there is no law, domestic or international, that justifies such an action. They didn't have an order impounding the building, they didn't ask for permission from its owner and there was no military or security justification for their action. They were driven by their sense of military superiority and their conviction that at no time would they ever be held accountable for their illegal action. The children, Tala and Aziz, also woke up to find their house, their private space where they sit for breakfast in the kitchen, occupied by strangers, armed men who were giving orders to their father. Then they took him away. At gunpoint. They put the gun in his back and forced him to go with them up to the neighbours. He was their human shield.

The children began to cry. They asked their mother, 'Where are the soldiers taking our father?' Hanan was distracted, worried about her husband. She wanted to protect him, to scream at the soldiers. She neglected the children because she was asking the soldiers who stayed behind where the others had taken her husband. '*Sheket* [shut up],' they snapped at her contemptuously. She had no right to ask, or address them in any way. She should remember her place and remain silent, invisible and out of their way. They had work to do. The children didn't like to see their mother shouted at and they began to cry. 'Where have they taken our father?' they asked. She tried to comfort them, but it was no use. They could see how her bosom was heaving and her fingers shaking. The soldiers were annoyed at the children's cries and pointed their guns at them to silence them. The children held back their tears and waited. It was an agonizing wait. They had all been forced into one room now and told that they couldn't leave it. A soldier was placed at the door to guard them. This was no longer their house. The minutes dragged. Samer had not returned. Hanan sat in silence, sweating. Where have they taken him? Why couldn't they at least tell her? Time passed slowly, oh so slowly.

When Samer returned, seemingly hours later, he was as pale as a lemon, withdrawn, looking parched. He had had to stand ahead of the soldiers as they forced open all the doors in the building. The soldiers had nudged him with their guns, abused him and taken liberties with his person as they had done with his house. Samer could feel the fear in the soldier who had stuck the gun in his back from the way he twitched whenever a new door was opened. He knew that none of his neighbours was armed or would put up a fight. This was a building of professionals, people who work in business who have families, who are uninvolved in politics or warfare. He worried only that any loud sound or sudden movement might frighten the soldier into pulling the trigger of the gun aimed at him.

Tala needed to go to the toilet. She was crying. 'Come, I'll take you,' Hanan told her. But Tala shrugged her shoulders, indicating that she did not want to move. Unlike her brother, she is thin and fragile, but she is strong-willed.

'Don't be afraid,' her mother told her, 'I'll get permission from the soldiers.'

As soon as Hanan said this she realized the absurdity of the situation that she should need to ask for permission from an Israeli soldier to take her daughter to the toilet in her own house. But she was willing to do it for the sake of her daughter.

Tala still shrugged her shoulders. Her great discomfort was obvious and yet she was afraid to pass the soldier and be close to his frightening gun. She wanted to stay in the corner, as far away from him as possible. Her mother began to tell her a story, but Tala wasn't listening. She whispered to her mother, 'Turkey is very nice.' The summer before they had been there on vacation.

'Yes, I know,' said her mother, 'but why?'

'There is the sea and the pool. I like it there.'

Hanan understood the message her daughter was trying to communicate: why are we here, not there? She continued to try and distract her with the story. But it was no use. Tala's world had crumbled. She could no longer find security in it. Her hero was her older brother, whom she imitated in every way. And both children had their father as their hero, whom they admired and saw as God almighty. Now Tala's first hero was in the corner, afraid and intimidated, and their father, the big hero, was being pushed around and humiliated.

The soldiers now began to bring down all the neighbours, packing them in the same room in Samer's house. They all sat in silence, breathing heavily. At this point the children must have wondered what was going on, what was going to happen next. Then a tall, fair soldier barged into the room and began to scream at their upstairs neighbours whose house he had just finished searching. He used Arabic swearwords that Samer would never have allowed his children to hear.

'It was you who shot at us when we came into the building,' the soldier said, opening wide his hand. 'I found these bullet shells in your house. You bring your son and come with me. I know how to deal with your kind, you bastard.'

'Wait a minute,' the man said. 'These are your bullets. My daughter collected them from the garden after you were here the last time.'

'You're a filthy liar,' the soldier snapped.

'No, I'm not, and I will prove it to you. Take me up to my apartment and I'll show you.'

The two went up together, the soldier pointing his gun at the man. A little while later their neighbour returned with a piece of paper, a little note written by one of the Israeli soldiers who had occupied their apartment during the last incursion into Ramallah. A soldier had knocked down a plant and had left the soil on the ground. Another had lifted the plant with its roots and placed it in water to save it from dying. He had left a piece of paper on which he had written in English, 'Sorry for the mess. I hope we meet in better times. Stay away from the windows. The IDF.'

This satisfied the soldier and they left the neighbour alone. Now there was quiet. But the soldiers were not budging. The children began to wonder whether they were going to stay in their house for ever. How, then, would they be able to go to sleep with the soldiers in the house, or play with their games or watch television or go to school? The soldiers smoked all the time. The house was full of smoke. But Tala did not dare tell them what she tells her father when he smokes the occasional cigarette, holding her little finger up to close one nostril: 'My nose closes when you smoke.'

The soldiers stationed in Samer's house were a mixed group. Hanan could tell the good ones from the bad by the manner in which they held their guns. The good ones pointed them down to the floor, the bad ones pointed them at the Palestinians all the time they sat with them in their living room.

I have always felt paternal towards Samer, who is seven years younger. Now he was in such danger and I could do nothing. How will this end? I was petrified with worry when I heard what happened in another house that soldiers had taken over. A young man of eighteen had asked permission to use the toilet.

When another man returned from a visit to the toilet with clear signs of having been beaten, the young man changed his mind. 'But you must,' the soldier standing guard at the door said. When he still refused, he was dragged out and beaten on the head. The soldier allowed the mother to call an ambulance only after two hours had passed, by which time the man had bled to death.

My brother and his family were not my only immediate concern. I was also thinking of my mother. She was seventy-five and living with a helper. Otherwise she was alone. She's a long-term sufferer of high blood pressure. A few years ago she underwent a major brain operation. What if she should need medical assistance? What if her house was shelled? But I could do nothing to help anyone, and my earlier efforts with officialdom had come to nothing.

My private, orderly world had crumbled. Cruel, irrational politics was all around me, refusing to leave me alone. The events of the past few years had soured relations between us and the Israelis to the point that even their reservists did not see us as human beings.

Last December the army had made their first limited incursion into Ramallah since the signing of the Interim Agreement in 1995. They occupied my neighbourhood but not my brother's. Aziz continued to phone me, asking to visit. I knew that he wanted to satisfy himself that I was not in any danger. I was not allowed to use my car, so I walked down and met him beyond the temporary checkpoint placed by the army opposite the gate of the UNRWA community college. I tried to convey to him that there was nothing to be afraid of. As we walked back towards my house, I told my nephew that the tank has a small compartment inside, like a tiny room. 'Would you like to see it?' I asked him. When we passed the tank, I was glad to see that the soldier had lifted the side door and was sitting outside on the pavement, sunning himself and reading his newspaper. This made the tank seem less forbidding.

'Come,' I told Aziz, 'let us look inside the little room. Shall we ask permission from the soldier to go inside? What do you think?'

My nephew looked at me with his large intelligent eyes as though I were utterly mad. 'No,' he said, with a knowing grin to indicate that he knew I could not be serious, and tried to get me to walk faster away from the tank.

Now I hoped that our small excursion during a less tense time might have prepared him to deal with this more vicious incursion.

After spending many hours sick with worry, I began to tell myself that my brother was a strong man who would be able to endure. It had taken him a long time to get settled, when I continued to feel protective towards him. But now he has pulled through. He has a happy, stable marriage, he is raising a family and is doing very well in work. I must have trust in him. My mother is the more serious cause for concern. Yet despite her physical frailty, she is psychologically strong. During her life with my father she was totally dependent on him. But since he was murdered, in 1985, she has learned to manage on her own. I always thought of her as a frail woman. I have since learned how wrong I was. She is capable and resilient. Strong-minded, she relishes the company of others and is able to get along with all sorts of people. She is sustained by her imaginative mind and strong sense of humour. I must trust that she too would be able to endure. What choice have I got? I cannot reach them. I am powerless. I had thought it would be possible to be left alone in my country to live my own life, without the need for contacts, for support, for relations with the powerful. I told myself this will pass. Now it looks so dangerous and full of unexpected perils, but it will pass, as the many other similar storms have passed, as the 1967 war, the Gulf War, as the dangers of life during 1982 and the seven years of the Intifada. I must heed the lessons of the past, must not lose my cool, must not get into a rage, must not resort to negative emotions. I must try and lead as orderly a life amidst all this chaos as is possible. Above all I must not begin to lose respect for myself by wasting my time and getting myself in such a state as to be unable to think, write and do useful work. This is life here: constant trauma, tragedy, catastrophe, violence, brutality and stupidity. If I am to be paralysed, then this would be the permanent state of my life, for the interim periods of quiet are brief and far apart.

* * *

Clearly the invasion two weeks ago had been only a precursor. Then the army had entered the outskirts of Ramallah, concentrating their attacks on the surrounding refugee camps. The centre of the town, including Arafat's headquarters, was left untouched. The armed men thought they could again find refuge there. Some were hiding in various buildings in and around the centre. They should have known that the Israeli army, like any good army, would never repeat the same tactic twice. This time they came from several positions; they used tanks but also entered on foot. They surrounded the centre and concentrated their attacks there. They met with limited resistance. At a certain level the decision must have been taken not to defend the town. Still, there were some who fired at the soldiers. Whenever shots were fired, the army retaliated with barrages of fire from tanks and heavy machine-guns.

The centre, where most of the action was taking place, is not far from the Manara roundabout with the plastic lions where, during the last incursion, the Palestinian fighters took shelter. Five of the main arteries of the town meet here. One of these, Irsal Street, leads after less than a mile to Arafat's headquarters. Another, which is perpendicular to it, is Main Street, the street of my office. This is a two-lane road with shops on each side. Close to the middle of this street are two five-storey buildings opposite each other, built during the Oslo years. One of these is called the Natshe Building. It has six floors, the higher awkwardly overhanging the lower. This building is next to the Quaker Meeting House, which has a spacious front yard with seven old pine trees. In the Natshe Building a number of armed men were hiding. Some of them must have shot at the Israeli army. The retaliation was brutal. Further down the street, just past my office, is a limestone building with round soft corners and large French windows called the Arizona. It has shops on the ground floor and offices on the upper floors. One of them is the Teachers' Development Centre, established by a friend of mine who was spending the year at Stanford. This building is next to a car park. It also has the office of FIDA, one of the PLO factions. Further north is another building and then, at the top of the hill, the once famous Ramallah Grand Hotel, with its large and beautiful pine-tree garden.

Halfway between the Natshe and Arizona buildings is the

corner of Post Office Street. Just near the top of this street is a car park, at the end of which is the Midan Building. This has a shopping centre and offices, including those of the Ministry of Finance, as well as some private residences. It was around this area that much of the fighting and bombardment took place. All these buildings were heavily damaged. My mother lives just behind the Midan Building.

But the initial heavy attack was directed against the Muqata (the compound where Arafat was staying). The compound was attacked from different sides. Several tanks were stationed on Irsal Street, which begins from the Manara roundabout. These bombarded the western wall bordering the pavement. The main gate was also destroyed. Further down, closer to the Manara, another tank was shelling the southern end of the compound containing the building that had served, during the Israeli occupation, as what was called the Civil Administration. Most Palestinians over the age of twenty-eight remember the humiliation they had to endure when they went there for the different kinds of permits required by the occupation authorities. Having destroyed these two outer walls and the corner building, the tanks now proceeded inside the compound and began their attacks on the old British-built cement structure, the Tegart. This had been used by the Israeli army as the headquarters of the military governor of Ramallah, the military court and prison. Built with fortified concrete, it was being gutted by the bombardment. Having broken the main door, the soldiers entered the building and began searching it room by room, demolishing the partition walls and vandalizing it. But Arafat was not there. Several years ago a further annexe had been built for him by the Palestinian Authority. This was a limestone building to the

23

north of the main structure. It was attacked from the east, causing some of the cornerstones to fall. The walls on that side of the compound were brought down and the tanks were now inside the section of the compound surrounding the building where he and his associates were staying. It now appeared that they were going to enter this building and take the Palestinian leader hostage.

A number of Palestinian politicians were interviewed in the wake of the attack on Arafat. From the way they spoke I thought they were with him in the compound. Then it became apparent that they were trying to take undeserved credit for their solidarity with the leader. In fact they were not in any danger. They were outside, planning future political moves. A palace coup seemed to be taking place just as the 'palace' was being shelled. Figures who never were known for their willingness to comment publicly on events were now vociferous. Developments were taking place quickly. I was aware that the Israeli government was holding large sums of money belonging to the Palestinian Authority. Should it choose, it could transfer these to any new leadership that might arise with its blessing and support.

The attack on Arafat had hardly begun and the aspirants were beginning to stir and get visibility. This made me wonder whether there was an Israeli/American plan for Arafat's succession. The way the fighting around his compound was taking place, it would be easy for the Israelis to claim that Arafat was killed in crossfire.

Heavy bombardment was also directed at the Arizona Building. Apparently those guarding the FIDA office were trapped inside. They didn't seem to have clear instructions what to do. Should they surrender? But how? If the army should barge in and find them armed, they would surely kill them. Should they then defend themselves? But against tanks?

The tanks were stationed in the car park to the east of the building. They were bombarding it with a continuous barrage, as though this civilian building was a formidable fortification. A number of families live in the buildings around the car park. They were petrified with fear. The noise was horrendous. They worried that ricochet bullets would damage their houses and endanger their families. They began to vacate their houses and take refuge with neighbours living further away. But everywhere in the centre there was bombardment and danger. People could move only within their building. If they went out to the street they risked their life. They had the worst time. They had never experienced anything like this before.

As the bombardment continued, one of the three guards at the FIDA office decided to escape. He threw himself from the second floor. The army saw his body fall and they went after him. The ambulance came too, as did members of the foreign contingent, who were making themselves available to help the wounded. Among the foreigners was a member of the European Parliament, Louisa Morgantini. She tried to help the ambulance workers carry the injured man, but the army wouldn't allow it. A scuffle ensued and the man was carried away by the army medics. Fortunately the fall did not prove fatal and his life was saved. The two others inside the building were shot dead.

The journalists were doing an excellent job covering all the action as it was happening. One of these working for Nile Television wanted to get a better view of the events taking place at the Muqata. They were moving their van closer to the demolished wall when an Israeli sniper shot the driver of the van.

'Were you hit?' the journalist in front asked the driver.

Faintly, almost apologetically, the driver answered in the affirmative.

I was watching the scene on television and noticed the hole that the bullet had made in the windscreen of the van.

'Let's get down. Quickly, quickly,' the reporter screamed as he helped the man out of the van. The driver lay on the ground. The reporter leaned over him and placed his finger across the hole in his neck. He was trying to keep the blood in as he screamed, 'Ambulance, ambulance. For God's sake, send for an ambulance.' His screams were getting louder and more desperate, until he was shrieking, 'For God's sake, ambulance, ambulance. Ambulance. We need an ambulance here.'

The wounded man now lifted his head. He wanted to say something. The reporter stopped screaming and listened, 'Take care of my wife,' he whispered.

'By God, I will. I will,' his friend said, with pathos in his voice, and resumed his desperate calls for an ambulance.

It was like watching a heart-wrenching, superbly acted movie. But it was not. It was real and it was all happening live before my eyes. I couldn't help crying as I watched.

But this episode was only a filler. The main focus remained all day on Arafat. Would he be captured and expelled? What would this mean to the future of the Palestinian struggle?

∗ ∗ ∗

The telephone never stopped ringing. Everyone inquiring about my safety. My mother was reporting a lot of shooting around her house. My brother reported that the soldiers had allowed the neighbours back to their apartments but were staying in his. All day two soldiers stayed in his living room, guarding the front and kitchen doors. My brother and his family have now been allowed to stay in their living room. As Samer attempted to distract his six-year-old son with the Playstation on television, the soldiers watched.

The man who lives in the apartment opposite my law office called. He told me that several armed Palestinian men on the run had tried to open the street door of the office. They used a crowbar, which succeeded in bending the strong metal door but it would not open. They left and went looking for somewhere else to hide. Above our office two new floors are in the process of being built. They must have wanted to use these for sanctuary.

I read over the e-mail that our friend Islah is desperately worried about Jad, a young man in the security forces who is a friend of her son. She had offered to keep him at her house. He stayed the night that the Israeli army entered Ramallah, then left. She got a frantic call from him around noon, telling her he was trapped in a building surrounded by the army. He wanted her to send the Red Cross to save him. She tried her best, but failed. Then all contact with him ended.

The more I saw and heard, the angrier I became. What sort of political and security authorities leave their people, civilians and officials, stranded like this? The decision not to resist the Israeli attack was sensible. Why were some allowed to violate it? And why had those armed by the Authority been left to fend for themselves, moving from one empty apartment block to another? There seemed to be a Palestinian strategy neither for war nor for peace. Many opportunities were missed. We continue to suffer one setback after another, one disaster after another. And we are expected to endure in silence, and at the end of every defeat express our understanding and suspend reality by turning the defeat into a victory. How many more such victories can we endure?

In the old city of Ramallah, we saw the army tying the hands of a group of young men in civilian clothes with a plastic rope used to wrap boxes. They were lined on the ground, crouching with their heads down. The reporter asked one of them who he was. 'We are all Birzeit University students,' he answered. 'They came to our house, destroyed our books and computers, and took us with them.'

Then we saw the army ordering a large number of uniformed men to pull up their shirts to show that they had nothing wrapped around their waists. What humiliation for members of the security force to have to reveal their naked flesh before the cameras of the world.

30 March

Yesterday towards the afternoon I heard a short click and the electricity went out.

Without electricity the house began to die: the water pressure, the heat (the weather was bitingly cold), the lights, the computer, the telephone, even the comforting sound of the BBC news on the hour announcing the most extraordinary events in that reasonable tone of voice. All my electrical gadgets were off. It was quiet inside the house. It was also quiet outside; there seemed to be a lull in the shooting. Earlier I had heard extensive tank movements around the house. I wondered nervously if the army had switched off the electricity from our neighbourhood in preparation for a special operation. The twilight began to get faint and the outside became more hostile and uncertain. I looked for candles. If the army should pay me a visit tonight, would I hear them without the doorbell?

The outside was a cold, dark, gloomy world swarming with tanks and soldiers bent on destruction and terror. And I was alone in my house, my unprotected fortress. I wrapped myself in my cardigan and sat by the fireplace, one hand holding the manuscript of the novel I was working on and the other a candle. When I moved, the wax dripped over my papers. Then I began hearing sporadic shooting, sometimes sounding like automatic machine-gun fire, sometimes like shell fire. How am I to tell? After living all these years in a war zone, I still refuse to learn to distinguish between different kinds of gunfire. Sometimes the crackle of guns sounded like the drilling that was so prevalent during the Oslo years, as one building after another was constructed, filling the empty hills around my house. I sat alone and thought that if the army should come, I would have no option but to open the door. Otherwise the soldiers would explode it.

How many of them would come? Samer says his house has thirty soldiers. Would they let me go with them as they searched or would they kick me into a corner and throw my books and papers off the bookshelves? Would they make me crouch and stamp my back with their boots, as I have heard they've done to others? But these were younger men. Perhaps I would be handled differently in deference to my fifty years. But then I don't look like a respectable middle-aged man. Living alone now in the house, I'm looking altogether so shabby that they might refuse to believe that I am the owner of this house and take me for a squatter. After I prove to them that I am the rightful owner, they would ask me to open all the doors, including the garage door, and there they would see the old refrigerator that I have been meaning for the past ten months to send to our winter home in Jericho as soon as the roads opened. The bags of the chemical fertilizer I keep for the plants and the smell of the insecticides for the rose bushes might make them suspect that this is a bomb factory. I'm told all it takes to prepare bombs are fertilizers, some sugar and nails. I have all three ingredients in my house.

The garage walls are lined with metal shelves. I keep copies of my diaries in boxes on these shelves. If the soldiers want to be mean, they would force me to bring down these heavy boxes. Once they are on the floor, they would ask me to dump out all their contents. There goes the chronicle of my years in human rights. Then up again to bring another box. My experiences of the Gulf War are next dumped before them. The soldiers are not interested in print. They're looking for guns and I have none. I try to plead that it would be difficult to sort all these papers again, but they are not impressed. They want to check all the boxes. I could see my life scatter before me. Down come the diaries of the early years of the occupation, long before these men were born, then the 1970s, 1980s and 1990s. All are now mixed in one large pile between the car and the old refrigerator, words describing the most intimate experiences mixed with descriptions of the horrors and brutality of three decades of occupation. But none of these would interest the young soldiers. To them all Palestinians are one. They all hate and want to destroy them.

I had stopped reading as I nursed my fantasies of the horrors that awaited me. My candle had burned down. I extinguished what was left of it, felt my way to bed and slept without being disturbed.

✳ ✳ ✳

Today, Saturday, the second day of the invasion, I have been trying to take more control over my life. I spent hours working on revisions of my novel. Then I was called by *The New York Times* and asked to submit an article for their op-ed page. As I thought of what to write, I realized how angry I was feeling about what was taking place. The Israeli army does not recognize our humanity. The Arab world does not really know what we've been through. They see it all as black and white, good and evil. They are not attuned to the shades of grey, to the times when there was potential for a different sort of relation with our enemies. They are helping bring back the heroic rhetoric and empty talk. Watching these Arab satellite stations reporting on what was happening to us, I was sometimes swept away. Only today, without television, with just the sound of the guns outside, was I able to understand my double role. Being in danger myself, I was the subject of the television coverage. Yet at the same time, watching all this on television, I was also the viewer who followed the live coverage as though it were a narrative that was happening to others. I was the viewer and the viewed; the object and the subject. The more I reflected on my double role, the more annoyed I felt at how the war, the subject of our suffering, was being turned into the stuff of drama for Arab viewers. Only today, with the drama turned off, was I able to go back to my senses.

I spent a long time pacing around the house for exercise and reflection. The events of the last day and a half began to make more sense. First, the sight of all these proud men with arms. They must have concluded that any invasion would be like the last one. It would leave them a place of refuge around Arafat's headquarters. But the Israeli army this time left them no place to hide. Most of them surrendered. A few were killed; the others were arrested, along with multitudes of unarmed civilians. Some tried their luck at shooting at the tanks, and the damage the army caused to those buildings from which the shots were fired was tremendous. How could those responsible have allowed it to get to this point? They could neither restrain the population nor prepare it for the consequences, or even warn it of what was coming. As a result we, the civilians, find ourselves at the mercy of a vengeful army.

✳ ✳ ✳

Over these past nineteen months since the Intifada began my space has been constantly narrowing. First it became too dangerous to go for walks in the hills around Ramallah, then I stopped being able to drive to Israel, then driving between the Palestinian towns and villages was prohibited. Now I cannot even step outside the door of my house. The perimeters of my house are all that is left for me of Palestine that I can call my own, and even this is not secure.

✳ ✳ ✳

The Israeli army, I heard, is claiming to have found documents incriminating the Palestinian leadership and linking it to the importation of arms. Surely this cannot be a big find. Israeli intelligence must have an abundance of such evidence. I know how the Palestinian leadership operates from my experience with the negotiating delegation in Washington, DC. The leadership in Tunis would speak to the delegation on the telephone. They would instruct it to take the most extreme positions and refuse all Israeli offers. Of course they were aware that the telephones were tapped. They spoke in such extreme negative terms precisely for the benefit of those tapping the phone line. This was their way of passing to the US administration the message that, unless they were accorded political recognition, they would continue to instruct their delegates in Washington to take the most extreme positions. They wanted the US to know that without PLO recognition no agreement with Israel could be reached.

The message was received. The tactic was successful. The PLO got the recognition it sought. In return they agreed in Oslo

33

to drop the condition that had stalled the negotiations in Washington for a freeze on the construction of Jewish settlements.

The Palestinian leadership always appreciated that the armed struggle was not an end in itself. All that the Palestinians could do was poke at the gargantuan Israeli body. They couldn't bring it to suffer serious damage. Armed struggle was dangled as a threat. Its power lay in its nuisance value. Political standing would be accorded only to those with the power to dangle this threat.

It could also well be the case that even if the Palestinians had tried, they would not have been successful in conducting clandestine operations away from the watchful eyes of the powerful Israeli intelligence service and the extensive network of Palestinian collaborators plugged into the various levels of the Palestinian administration and society. Well before this military occupation took place, Israel must have had an abundance of copies of faxes incriminating the Palestinian leadership. When it suited its purposes, it used these to make a case against the Palestinian Authority, as in the *Karin A* arms ship. I cannot believe that one of the strategic objectives of this invasion was for the Israeli authorities to capture more evidence to condemn and implicate Arafat. They never lacked it.

✱ ✱ ✱

When I didn't pace I read. Reading kept my mind off ugly musings. But the best cure for ending these tedious thoughts that I was excavating from a troubled past would be sleep. Tonight I didn't want to worry about the possibility that the soldiers would visit me. As long as they were not inside my house, I decided to take them out of my mind and went to sleep.

31 March

The electricity continued to be out until noon today. When it returned, I felt my house come back to life. The water pressure tank sighed with relief as it filled up again, the answering machine on the telephone announced that it was off, the toilet flush gurgled and began to fill up, the heating boiler and refrigerator started their low murmurs – all wonderful sounds. Life was looking up. I was suddenly so happy and light-headed. Then the telephone rang and my mother reported that the Chamber of Commerce building next to her house was on fire. She was worried that the fire would spread to her house. What could I do? How could I help? I tried to assure her that the fire needn't spread, because our houses are of limestone, not wood, and stone does not catch on fire. I didn't want her to panic.

But I was not going to go back to television watching during the day. I turned it off, went to my desk, finished revising my manuscript and sent it off by e-mail to my publisher. Then I felt relieved. Should anything happen to me, should the army break into my house and destroy my computer, my manuscript would be safe.

In the evening I went back to news monitoring. I learned that at three-thirty in the afternoon a significant development had taken place at the Muqata that might have saved the life of the Palestinian leader. A group of sixty foreigners had managed to find their way inside Arafat's last refuge. These were from among the ninety Grassroots International Protection and International Solidarity Movement members in Ramallah, the foreigners Mustafa Bargouti had told me about when we met in the street on Thursday.

With destruction all around him and tanks on every side of his compound, Arafat was still holding his fort. The Israeli tanks had come as close as possible to his office but had stopped short of killing him. It was quite a spectacle. Out of his bunker, he was able to pass the following message, which was broadcast on television: 'They want me a prisoner, an exile or a dead man, but I shall be a *shaheed* [martyr].' The last word was repeated three times in a descending tone: *shaheed, shaheed, shaheed*. After I heard this message I tried to analyse it. The pronoun 'they' refers to the enemy. The Israelis are after me, but I resist. I shall escape from their clutches and shall not let them turn me into a prisoner or an exile. I shall also define my own death. It may be death all the same, but not on their terms, because I intend to be a martyr.

My neighbour, a shopkeeper in his late middle age who crept from his adjoining house to visit me, said of him, 'What a man! He is in his seventies and can stand to be under such attack and without food or medical care. He is extraordinary. I tell you, he has entered history.'

Arafat's message was being repeated every hour. Samer's soldiers would listen to it and every time the words '*shaheed, shaheed, shaheed*' came on they all sang mockingly along: '*shaheed, shaheed, shaheed*'. They found it very amusing.

In some neighbourhoods soldiers incorporated the words into their call for curfew, which they prefaced with the address Arafat uses to extol his people: 'O heroic people, curfew is declared. Whoever violates it will be a *shaheed, shaheed, shaheed*.'

Other soldiers mimicked the high voice of the female correspondent of the Al Jazeerah satellite station in their call for curfew: 'Curfew is declared, Sherin Abu Akleh, Al Jazeerah.'

The soldiers had plenty of opportunities to think of ways to vary their calls for curfew, for it has still not been lifted for a single hour since it was first imposed at dawn on Friday. The army do not seem to be too concerned with the pressing needs of the population for bread and milk for their children and medicines.

* * *

An inauspicious hike seems to have afflicted the voice register of some of our eminent leaders since the start of the occupation. I have been noticing that when interviewed on television they no longer charm us with their deep gravelly bass voices. They've moved up the scale. Also their earlier bravado talk about their plans to stand firm has been replaced by a denunciation of the Israeli army: 'They are like the Tartars. They steal and rob and have gone to banks and left the doors open. They have taken money from the moneychangers and jewellery from the shops in Ramallah. Not a single house they entered they didn't rob. They take all that can be carried and leave nothing. They are making massacres. They are savages.'

As I listened, I felt glad that the town was under a strict curfew, otherwise we might have seen a mass exodus to escape from the clutches of these Tartars. This was not the most responsible message to pass on to a captive population.

* * *

In contrast to the almost total absence of governmental bodies, the work of the non-governmental sector was of vital importance. The ambulance drivers of the Red Crescent society and Medical Relief were heroic. Also impressive was the speed with which information flowed. Then there was the effective use of the media by these relief organizations. When twenty-one people were trapped in the Daragmah Building on the same street as Arafat's headquarters, there was immediate mobilization. The Israelis were asking the men to surrender. But the men were worried that if they came out they would be massacred. An ambulance was sent to take the wounded. One of the foreign contingents accompanied it. As the ambulance approached very slowly, in full view of the large number of tanks, a brave American middle-aged woman continued to announce its approach with the loudspeaker. It took hours for it to get there. The news that there was this number of men trapped in the building, afraid for their lives, was made known throughout the world. Whether or not it was the ambulance and the broadcast that were instrumental in preventing a massacre from taking place would never be known. The news the day before that five people were killed at close range in another building where they had been trapped made those involved with the Daragmah incident believe that they had indeed prevented a massacre from taking place.

The Al Jazeerah correspondent in Bethlehem reported that the security forces there were expecting the Israeli army to occupy Bethlehem tonight. We heard from her that the security people have made preparations. In her words: 'They have made fortifications wherever they could, using what simple ammunition and weaponry they have at their disposal.'

The television phone-in programmes seem to be the only outlet left for people. There was a desperate call from someone who said he was trapped by the army with sixty people in a small space in a building in downtown Ramallah. The caller appealed for help. He asked rhetorically, 'Where are the Arab leaders to come and save us?' The Al Jazeerah announcer's sensible response was: 'The Arab leaders cannot do much for you in this particular instance. You need someone to bring you food and water.'

There is more rhetoric than ever and more bravado. The speakers are carried away with our illusory power. People from Arab countries are congratulating us for our heroism and shouting to the phone-in programme that they are willing, clamouring, praying to die for Palestine. One caller began to weep as soon as he was on air. 'How long will this go on?' he wanted to know, 'Where is Salah Ed Din? How can we stand to see what is happening and not act?' And on and on. Once again Palestine was being turned into a symbol.

As usual, Arafat had upstaged everyone. Many were asking on the air, 'How can the Arab leaders stand to see this Arab leader under siege for the third day and do nothing? How can this be?'

These are, of course, legitimate questions. Yet few are showing concern for the plight of ordinary people, whose needs are not being met, whose lives are being destroyed. It is well and good to be concerned with the poetics, the representation, the rhetoric, but we are all in need of fresh bread, which we have not been able to get for three days.

Yesterday Samer and his family had a terrible time. They were in their living room, watching television. Israeli soldiers sat by the door, pointing their guns at them, when suddenly there was a news flash: another Palestinian bomb in a restaurant in Haifa. The anger of the soldiers sitting by the door in Samer's living room was palpable. Samer held his breath. The first thought on his mind was: what if any of these soldiers should lose a loved one in this attack? They would certainly pull the trigger and exact revenge against his family. Neither he nor his wife said anything. In a living room in Ramallah, Palestinian civilians and Israeli soldiers together watched the carnage inflicted by a Palestinian on Israeli civilians. Only later was Samer able to ask the soldiers if they had lost anyone. When they said that they had phoned their families and confirmed that no one they knew had been hurt, Samer breathed with relief.

1 April

It's the first day of April.

For a number of years my mother's old neighbour, the credulous Nabiha Salah, has been a candidate for an April fool joke. Last night she was found dead, alone in her house. She was one of my mother's oldest friends and my brother's godmother. Her only daughter's family are in Syria. They have never been able to come and visit her. My mother was worried that she might be buried without the religious rites. So she was on the case, trying to make arrangements. The priest said he was willing to perform the last rites. The problem was how to get the body to hospital and from there to the cemetery. And how to get permission for the gravediggers. Apparently this was why the hospital has been unable to bury the corpses they already have at the morgue. My mother was also told of another problem. The hospital was unwilling to receive another corpse because the morgue was full to capacity. Ramallah has had more casualties during this brief invasion than at any time in the last half-century of the many wars that have afflicted this country.

My mother said she wanted the telephone number of the governor of Ramallah. I asked her why.

'I want to call him,' she said.

'Don't bother,' I said. 'He can do nothing. He's trapped with Arafat in the Muqata.'

'What?' she asked. 'What's the use of being a governor if he doesn't act for the welfare of the people?'

I saw the back gate of my garden wide open this morning. Perhaps the army came in, inspected and decided not to go into my house. Today the centre of town is without electricity. Mother now doesn't have it.

* * *

It has turned out to be a beautiful, sunny first of April day. I cooked spaghetti (I felt like carbohydrates) and ate it alone. Penny has now arrived in Jerusalem but is still unable to make it to Ramallah. I did not want to hear any more news. I wanted to read. I sat on the couch in our lovely sunny sitting room with the new bookshelves and read. The sun was shining and for the first time since the invasion the birds were singing in the courtyard. The loudest was the bulbul, a bird with a deep expressive voice whose song sounds like a repetition of the phrase: I told you so, I told you so. The birds were happy because it had rained in the morning. They can take little baths in the puddles. My grandmother used to say, '*Shatwit nisan ibtihi el insan*' (The spell of rain in April revives man).

I have spent happy years in this house. We finished building it in 1996. I had been determined never to build a house. The agony over the loss of the family home in Jaffa convinced me it was better not to develop attachments to property. But when the Oslo deal was signed in 1993, I expected we would enter a period of upheaval. I thought the only way to survive would be to have a place of refuge to return to at the end of the day. How right I was.

I have not missed involvement in public matters. I much

prefer a detached life. After thirteen years of human rights activism, the climax of my public involvement was advising the Palestinian negotiating team in Washington, DC. I did my best to alert the delegation to the legal pitfalls. When the Oslo Accords, with which I had nothing to do, were published, I was dismayed by the abandonment of many of the legal and human rights issues on which I had worked for years. The only effective struggle I could foresee would be of a political nature, but this was not for me. I stepped aside, concentrated my energies on my legal practice and writing, and lived with Penny on borrowed time in Palestine – the happiest years of my life.

I had made a conscious decision to be a self-exile here. For a number of years this was possible. Both the Israeli and Palestinian authorities left me alone. Now my respite seems to be coming to an end. The Israeli authorities are returning with a vengeance, sending their army to remind me that a Palestinian does not have the luxury of living quietly, creatively, in his own country. He will be chased, choked and hounded.

***

Last night twenty soldiers slept in my brother's living room. Fortunately this was their last night there. One of them was a paramedic who may have had his doubts about the expediency of the army's operation. He had earlier told my brother that he thought well of the Palestinians, 'It's just that you have bad leadership.'

Samer responded by telling him what he thought of the Israeli leadership.

Before the officer left Samer's house he told my brother, 'You know, both our leaders are lousy. It is only because of them that we are fighting each other.'

'I agree,' Samer responded, 'but I cannot help thinking that we are not equal. You're a soldier and I'm a civilian.'

'Look,' the soldier said. 'When we first arrived here, three men shot at us. It didn't take much for us to find and kill them. It was obvious that they were not properly trained. All they had were simple guns that stood no chance against our tanks. I cannot understand why they do it. Do you know that I went through rigorous training and learned how to shoot to kill from twenty-one different positions? How could these men have expected to win against us?'

Samer had one question to ask this soldier. He wanted to know whether the army would be taking over his house every time they invaded Ramallah.

'Your house is marked on our map with a number and a circle. We will come back to it every time we return to Ramallah,' the officer assured him.

When Samer conveyed this to Hanan, they put their heads together and began to consider how and when to emigrate. They had wanted to think of this as a passing episode, but after what they had heard it was no longer possible. Their sense of security had vanished. They felt they had the house to themselves only until the next time, whenever that might be. Any morning they might wake up to find the Israeli army in their living room, taking over their house and terrorizing their children. This was no way to live.

✳ ✳ ✳

Mother has just called from the corridor, saying the sound of tank shelling was horrific. 'The glass in the house of my upstairs neighbour has just shattered,' she said. She was asking her helper for a chair. I heard her say, 'No, not this one, the one with the stiff back.' Then she told me, 'Once again history repeats itself. Here I am in the midst of the battlefield, just as I've been since I was a young student in boarding school in Haifa during the war, when the siren was right over my bed.'

Later she called again to say that the Midan Building near her house was on fire. The tanks were parked in the car park near my barber's house and they've been blasting at it as in a real war.

Mustafa Bargouti was on the BBC saying how violent and disrespectful the army was of doctors, the Red Cross and international observers. He said they are entering homes and places of work and destroying them. 'They have taken one of our doctors to use as a human shield. They used the foulest language against the internationals.' He ended by asking, 'Where is the international community, human rights and international law? This is a dark day for Israel, for the West, for the world.'

He was clearly disturbed, impassioned and angry.

There has been an escalation on all fronts since the Oslo Accords: more lethal weapons used against us, more anger, more people killed, more despair, more opportunities lost, more combat and more wars.

And certainly no less bravado and playing to the television audience. On Al Jazeerah they showed a Palestinian fighter from Bethlehem with his *kuffieh* covering his face except for holes for the eyes, declaring, 'The Israeli army will enter this town only over the dead bodies of all the men, the elderly and the children.'

I wonder whether better preparations have been made in Bethlehem for the fighters than has been the case in Ramallah.

2 April

I am beginning to feel like a prisoner in solitary confinement. My only privilege is my access to a telephone. My only exercise is pacing around the house. Still, I'm trying to use my time as well as I can, reading and writing. I use my provisions sparingly so as not to run out.

I was born four years after my family was forced out of their home in Jaffa. We never had much to waste. It is not difficult to revert back to former habits. I noticed I am back to peeling the stem of the cauliflower that I had been in the habit of throwing out. These practices are making me think of my paternal grandmother. She had been through a real famine during the later years of the First World War and told horror stories about this time. That must have been the worst period in this country's recent history. I hope I will not have similar stories to tell.

Last night was extremely noisy and tense. I was awakened many times by the sound of the bombing and shooting.

In the morning I learned that helicopter gunships were shelling the Preventive Security building. Samer reported that they are positioned right above his house. Every salvo they fired reverberated in the house. The children were miserable.

During all the previous attacks on Ramallah, the only installation that had remained untouched was the Preventive Security headquarters in the village of Beitunia, next to Ramallah. Its head had kept his men out of the fighting and the Intifada. This was why most of the employees, along with their families, were taking shelter in the building. Seven Hamas members wanted by the Israelis were also said to be in the prison of the Security building. Their incarceration had been carried out with the knowledge and consent of the Israelis, through their American interlocutors. The Israeli army may have believed that there were many more wanted people hiding in the building, or they may have simply used this as an excuse to justify their extensive brutal bombardment of it, in the course of fighting against Arafat and the sources of his power. Whatever the truth, the shelling there was as vicious and extensive as that of the Muqata.

It was not possible for the army to argue that this was a centre of terrorism. Among all Palestinian Authority organs, this was the best organized and the most restrained. It was also the most disciplined of the several security networks that had arisen in the wake of the Oslo Accords. Its forces were known to stay away from confrontations with the Israeli army. Their record of good and effective security coordination with the CIA and Israel was impressive. Why, then, was it being shelled in this vindictive manner? Surely if the objective was to get the seven wanted men, there were other less destructive ways to achieve this goal. The only answer I could find was that the army wanted to destroy all aspects of the Oslo deal. Israel was not looking for partners among the Palestinians, not on security, not on any other matter. It wanted to assume full and sole control over all aspects of Palestinian life.

Throughout the night the whole town was rocked with the horrendous reverberating sound of constant shelling, all directed at the building. Calls were being made to allow the Red

Cross to go into the area to take out the wounded, but the army refused to ease the shelling that went on all day unabated.

As the heavy shelling was continuing, one Palestinian official interviewed on Al Jazeerah was asked for his reaction to what was happening and what he thought should be done. His response was, 'There is only one way and this is the way of *sumoud*'. Then he added, 'Our *sumoud* is what would make all the difference. We shall not give in. We shall not surrender.'

The concept of *sumoud* has a lot of resonance for us. For a long time it was a Palestinian strategy for resisting Israel's attempts at emptying the occupied territories of their inhabitants.

I was very impressed with his heroic spirit until I realized that he was not one of the 400 said to be trapped inside the building. I was left to wonder how those enduring all this bombardment must have felt as they listened to someone outside the threatened building extolling the virtues of *sumoud*.

* * *

Two corpses of men shot near the famous ice-cream parlour in Ramallah, Rukab's, have been found. One of the dead was a cripple. The number of those killed in Ramallah is now twenty-seven. They still cannot be buried.

Members of the security forces who are from the Gaza Strip have been rounded up, put in a temporary prison camp and transferred to Gaza. I wondered whether those two young men who came to my office were among them. I wished it for them. Then at least they would not be among the twenty-seven dead. One of the Gazans was photographed with his hands and knees on the ground. It was not clear whether he was kissing the earth of Gaza, happy to be back safe and sound, or praying. Another sturdy young man said in an interview, 'They did many things to us. They beat us and let loose dogs on us.' Another, a more portly, older man, claimed that since Friday they had not had anything to eat. 'By God, nothing,' he said. 'We were not given any food. None whatsoever.'

Arafat is still holding on, besieged in his office. We see him in candlelight. We hear his food is running out. Our food is running out too, but it doesn't seem to matter. It is more important that we are provided with symbols and heroic stances than the satisfaction of our real-life needs. This tells something about us and our presumed role in the story.

✻ ✻ ✻

My brother has just told me that the curfew would be lifted from twelve to four. When I heard this I was surprised by my reaction. I was not thrilled. I even dreaded going out and meeting the tanks and the Israeli army back in full control of our town as they used to be before Oslo. Back to occupation and its frustrations, anger and emotional skirmishes. I had thought we had moved forward and would never again have Israeli soldiers in our midst. Then there was the prospect of seeing all the destruction without knowing what it was for and where we are going. I was like a prisoner who was in for too long, got comfortable and did not want to leave to meet and confront the changes that have occurred since he was incarcerated. He preferred to remain cooped up in his cocoon.

For four days I had not done any shopping. I had stocked up

before all this began but I was running out of bread, fresh vegetables, fruits and dairy products. I needed to go out and shop. I should not find refuge in my confinement.

I turned the ignition of the car. I had not used it for four days. I was relieved when it started. It was a rainy, misty day, unusual for April. I drove out of my garage, feeling strange to be moving out of the house. I noticed that the neighbour's car was in the garage. Had he not heard? Or was he, like me, reluctant to leave the house? I drove out of our small street up to Tireh Road. The UNRWA community college with its 800 boarding female students had its large blue gate completely shut. Why are they not letting the girls out to enjoy these brief hours of freedom with the curfew lifted? I drove down and realized mine was the only car on the road. I proceeded further into the mist towards the centre of town.

Then I met with an obstacle. A mound of earth was placed across the road just after the Boys Scouts' centre. As I considered what to do, I noticed that the large metal gate of the centre had been dislodged and parts of the wall demolished. A large pile of earth had been dumped, blocking the entrance. Should I drive over the mound on the road? It was, of course, very wet. What if my car got stuck? There wasn't anyone around to help me. I decided to turn back and find a side road.

The side roads were also empty. I took the one that winds around by the edge of the hill. Ramallah has lovely hills that now had wisps of mist wafting over them like a gossamer veil. I circled round and caught up with the main road. The roadside was strewn with debris. Israeli tanks had felled trees and grounded road signs. Cars lay flattened, the glass of their windscreens lying side by side level with their doors, bumpers and roofs in a decidedly final eternal slumber well beyond the point of ever returning to a three-dimensional state.

The tooth of the Israeli army bulldozer had dug into the tarmac of the road leading up to the centre of town and turned it. My car wobbled as I drove over the upturned tarmac. Why had they done this? There were more shops now on the side of the road and still not a single one of them was open. There were no other cars or pedestrians anywhere to be seen.

I argued with myself that perhaps only the centre of the town had been opened. Perhaps the owners of these shops were from out of town and could not come to open up because of the closure of the town. I had already come all this way; let me drive further up and see.

I was, of course, aware of the consequence of breaking curfew. The evening before I had seen the report on television of Malek's death, the nineteen-year-old from Jericho. He had been stranded in Ramallah at the restaurant where he was working when the invasion began. He had called a counselling centre in Jerusalem asking for advice. He told the counsellor that he was afraid because soldiers were on the roof of his building. She advised him to take deep breaths. But he was still afraid to be alone, so he decided to visit his neighbour across the street. As soon as he emerged from the restaurant the army sniper on the roof shot him dead. The television broadcast the pictures of the trail of blood leading all the way up the neighbour's stairs. The neighbour was a portly man who stood by the door, pointing down to show how Malek had made it up only the first three steps before collapsing. Could my brother have been mistaken about the curfew being lifted and I was risking my life? As a lawyer, the worst part of it was that if I was apprehended I would not be given an opportunity to explain. The soldiers would shoot or the tank would shell my car before I could tell them that I had no subversive intentions, it was my brother's mistake, I didn't deserve to die for it.

Then I saw a flickering light. Well, this was hopeful. I drove towards it in the thick mist. It turned out to be the traffic light, still flickering dutifully. It had turned red when I approached. I was the only car. Under these circumstances, do I wait or cross?

I was closer now to the centre and saw the gutted burned-up buildings that had been used as shopping centres and offices. Missiles had gone through their limestone walls, poking large holes, setting interiors ablaze. Now they were pitch black, modulated only by the veil of mist. And still I could not see anything open. My brother must have been wrong. The curfew had not been lifted. There I was in the centre of the town, now famous for Israeli snipers, and I was in violation of the curfew. If I should be spotted, I would surely be fired on. I turned and began my perilous drive back. I could hear my heart thumping.

This was a new experience of my town. It felt like a cold, hostile, unwelcoming place, in the grip of belligerent strangers who would see my simple act of driving along the old familiar streets of the town I have lived in all my life as subterfuge that could cost me my life. I turned into the side road, taking the same path I had come on to avoid the earth mound blocking the main street. I realized that out of habit I was putting on my turn signal. I tried to determine whether or not this was a good thing to do. Would it make me more visible in the mist and increase the likelihood of my being targeted? Yet if I drive showing fear, then any soldier I come across will be more inclined to shoot. Or are all these calculations inconsequential because, whoever I am, whatever my past, however I drive, I am a Palestinian breaking curfew and therefore a legitimate target for a merciless enemy in occupation of my town.

I was fortunate to have made it home safely from my first illegal excursion into town after the four-day curfew. An hour later came the genuine lifting of the curfew. Once again I left the house as reluctantly as the first time. This time I saw that my neighbour's car was not in the garage and Tireh Road was busy with nervous traffic. I went all the way to the centre. By the door of our office I found two big tanks looking so out of place in the narrow street that they entirely filled. They were like elephants taking a stroll in one's back garden. I approached, intending to check on the state of our office, but as I got close the tank's barrel started to move towards me menacingly. I turned my car around and went back.

On the side of several roads was the mangled metal of what used to be someone's car. It felt as though hooligans had been let loose in the town, given large machines and bulldozers and told to do whatever they liked. Over the Arafat banner in the main square the soldiers wrote in Hebrew, 'Your people have fled and deserted you.' Over the ferocious lion behind which the Palestinian men had crouched to shoot at Israeli soldiers during the last invasion, a solider had written in Arabic, 'Sharon', and painted in green on the other side of the head below the ears the star of David.

Later I thought how like a game it all is. One that is planned by evil men with big ambitions and huge destructive potential, and executed by infantile people who put the name of their evil leader on the head of a plastic lion.

But what was most distressing were the town's inhabitants.

They appeared as fellow prisoners let out for a brief exercise in the prison yard. They were no longer proud and victorious. They were now captured and guilty. Yet there was comfort in our stubborn survival. There was no time to talk, only a few words could be exchanged and congratulations at getting through safely so far.

Driving back, I was surprised that people still stopped at traffic lights. The tanks were parked only a few metres away and people were being observant of traffic regulations. Then, closer to my house, a large tank came speeding up the road and all of us quickly swerved to the side to avoid being hit and having our cars turned into mangled metal like the scores of cars we could see all along the way.

The shops had a fetid odour from the decaying foodstuff. There were no fresh products because no provisions had been allowed into the town. What, then, was the use of lifting the curfew?

It appeared to be more for the benefit of the dead. The army was concerned that the morgue be emptied, perhaps to make place for more dead and to avoid a public health disaster. But full funerals and burial at the cemetery were not allowed. So the orderlies at the hospital dug out two large holes in the car park and buried the men together in one hole and the women in another. Among the corpses was one of the guards at the FIDA office in the Arizona Building. His young wife was summoned to bid him farewell before his shrouded body was put in the ground. Jad, the young security officer, was left alone in the morgue. His mother had finally been contacted and wanted him sent to Jenin for burial. The events of the last day of his life had now become known. He and his friends had left the building they were hiding in when they heard the rumour that the army were massacring anyone they found inside abandoned buildings. Near the Arizona Building they were spotted and shot at. He was the only one to die. Islah's son had found his key chain in the spot where he fell. Her twenty-one-year-old son was there with her at the morgue. He kept repeating to his mother as he tried to come to terms with the finality of death, 'He died wearing the jacket I lent him, the green jacket. He died in my green jacket.'

* * *

The telephone just rang. 'I am calling everybody,' the voice of a woman acquaintance said. 'I knew you were alone. I should have called earlier. You were on my list of all the people I should call.'

All day today I could hardly sit down and begin to do something before I would get another call. I hate to place the telephone next to my desk. It would make my study at home feel more like my law office. I also thought that running from my study to the living room to get the telephone would be a form of exercise. But it was getting excessive. The telephone was ringing incessantly until I couldn't take it any more. I began to scream. Some people were commiserating as though I were terminally ill and my days were numbered.

But then the news spread that my spirits were low. So many of my family and friends felt it was their duty to call and cheer me up that I began to get even more calls.

Al Jazeerah has a programme called *Under Siege*, advertised as a portrayal of the experiences of the Palestinian population under the Israeli siege. The outside is doing its best to portray my life, to interpret my experience and existence. The Palestinian is to be both pitied and admired, to be helped and to help other Arabs by providing the inspiration and rhetoric to those who feel so impotent in their restricted world. He both accentuates their feeling of helplessness and relieves it. His life is a drama, a soap opera and yet reality, a reality programme on television to be watched and followed in real time. Not on his own terms but on the terms of the viewer, who brings to the film, to the experience, what suits, comforts and satisfies him. The enemy, the bad guy, is Israel and the devil is Sharon, who is hated without reservation. The way he speaks is despised, the way he looks, his arrogance, his smile that reveals the split between his front teeth, his being alive and victorious. Every gesture, word, the squint in his left eye is interpreted as a mark of great evil. The Palestinian is under his mercy and yet is also a match for him and stands up to him and therefore wins the admiration of the viewer.

I have always insisted on interpreting myself and now find all eyes of commiseration and pity turned on me and words of condolences directed at me, determining what it must be like for me without waiting to hear from me and allowing me to say my bit.

This perhaps was why, on top of everything I was going through, I felt so gloomy today. It was expected that I would be idle, available at all times to respond to the telephones of all the callers. When I became distressed, no one could consider the possibility that this was because of the endless disruptions to my work caused by these persistent calls, because I was not supposed or expected to have a life or work of my own.

My situation, I thought, was representative of Palestinian politics. Everyone felt they knew what was good for me and no one thought of asking.

3 April

All night I heard the Israeli bombardment of Palestinian institutions built after Oslo. In the morning I listened from my unprotected home to Palestinian officials with fancy titles, brigadiers, generals and ministers, trying to put an honourable gloss on this dishonourable defeat.

There were people who were stranded for days in buildings and shops without food surviving on dried chickpeas that they soaked in water and ate. The same problems that have existed over many years of this struggle persist. The armed struggle is merely waged for its nuisance value, not as a serious threat to Israel's existence. Israel cleverly utilizes it to justify extremist positions and measures taken against the Palestinians. The political negotiations are not conducted with any sense of strategy. I strongly doubt whether the Palestinian Authority as presently organized is capable of developing and following a strategy. Opportunities are missed and the wide international support and sympathy for our cause are never mobilized for good effect. The possibilities for alignments with the Israeli opposition to the right-wing policies of the government are completely wasted. The Palestinian bombings and armed attacks against Israeli civilians that clearly are politically damaging are not stopped. Irrational forces lead every aspect of our life at home and in the conduct of political and diplomatic affairs. We are a society that continues to be at the mercy of those who act out of their emotions of anger, frustration and hate.

* * *

The announcements made over the television regarding the Palestinian fortifications in Bethlehem and determination to fight to the last man have, of course, come to nothing. As in Ramallah, there was minimal resistance and the city has now been occupied. Some 200 people are trapped inside the Church of the Nativity. It is said that they have taken refuge there.

The Israeli army is proceeding to systematically destroy governmental and non-governmental offices. All five television and all five radio stations in Ramallah have been destroyed and vandalized. The most popular one, Watan, seems to have been kept partially functional, at least to the extent that it was possible for Israeli soldiers to hook it to a European pornographic station to 'entertain' the Palestinian population as they sit in their houses under a twenty-four-hour curfew.

But the documentation of what is taking place and dissemination of credible information are being carried out not by Palestinian officials but by individual effort. Penny has been dedicating all her time while in Jerusalem to the preparation with other colleagues of reports documenting the damage caused to local institutions. The cooperation with solidarity groups outside is strengthening. Except for these initiatives, only the Israeli version of events would be known.

An elderly woman in Ramallah died of a heart attack because the ambulance could not reach the house to take her away to hospital. I could not imagine (perhaps because I didn't allow myself to) what it would mean to live in a small house with a corpse that is going through the different stages of decomposition. In one of the reports from Bethlehem, they showed us a man sitting in a room with a corpse next to him. The television clip was without sound. We could see the man pointing to a wall that was puckered with bullet shots. Next to him, below the bed, on the floor with the back partly supported by the bed, was a dead man. His head was drooping to one side, almost touching the floor. Just watching this scene helped me to visualize our predicament and realize how blurred the distinction has become between conditions for the living and the dead.

The Israeli army has also entered Nablus and caused damage to the historic Turkish bathhouse and other historic buildings. There is a flurry of diplomatic activity that is getting nowhere.

Whatever amateurish fighting that had taken place in Ramallah has ended.

4 April

It has been raining, misty and cold. More like a winter day than a spring day in April. My grandmother would have been very pleased. I knew that many who were without heating were suffering. But for me the rejuvenation and moisture of the world outside my window were much more congenial as I sat in my house and wrote, looking out on a wet garden full of promise for a lovely colourful May. Had it been dry and everything in it dying, it would have been miserable.

Sidar had to leave her house when the invasion began and was staying with her daughter, Salwa. Just before the occupation she had bought a tin of white Nablus cheese, which she intended to preserve in brine for next winter. She tried to get back to her house to save the cheese from rotting but the army would not let her in. Now the cheese will spoil. When mother heard this she said, 'History repeats itself. In 1967, when Fuad and Labibeh [my aunt and uncle] left, they also had white cheese. Bahia and I tried to save it when the curfew was lifted.'

Wars and white cheese. The experience of the Israeli occupation in 1967 was entirely different from this one. The army was on its best behaviour. There was little fighting and hardly any destruction to Ramallah. The army entered very few houses to search them. With a bullhorn, the population was asked to bring any weapons they had to the bus stop in the old city and most complied. Our neighbour Bahu, a veteran hunter who had a hunting gun with a wooden stock inlaid with mother-of-pearl, had tears in his eyes as he walked past our house to the designated area to hand it over to the Israeli army. No snipers were stationed on high buildings with instructions to shoot to kill violators of curfew. It could have gone all sorts of ways. We could have learned to co-exist in two separate states side by side. Instead we still view our existence in this land as mutually exclusive of the other.

5 April

I got up early this morning. I began writing immediately after breakfast. Then I was told that the army would be lifting the curfew again from one to four. I went out. Most roads have been dug up and ditches created in the middle. Some roads were blocked, the town having been partitioned, it seems, into quadrants. The blockade consisted of a mound of earth dumped along the width of the road, on top of which was placed a garbage dumpster or, if none could be found, then a neighbour's car that was treated as a child's toy by the cynical army bulldozer, squashed and lifted up like a metal ball to decorate the road obstacle. Those to whom the car belongs would have watched from the window of their house the spectacle of the disgracing of their car, its destruction and use as a permanent exhibit atop the roadblock. To think that in addition to the painful ordeal of the occupation some have to endure the daily sight of their ruined car outside their window turned into mangled metal. And all this because Israeli soldiers had big machines with which to practise their weird form of fun against the property of unprotected civilians.

On my way up to town, just next to the office of Al Haq, the human rights organization I helped to establish in 1979, I was stopped by the soldiers and asked to open the boot of my car. As the soldier was inspecting it I stole a glance at the Al Haq office, now taken over by the army. In the first Intifada this was where

I spent most of my time, helping to document Israeli violations of human rights. I had been confident that our struggle was going to bring an end to the Israeli occupation. It was not to be. Nine years later we are back once again to full occupation.

The Chamber of Commerce is blackened. The Midan Building has part of the wall of the second floor demolished. Mother must really have had a bad time of it. And so did the family of my barber, who lives down by the car park.

There were nervous movements among the people as they scurried to get bread. At the Catholic Church they were distributing rations, a box of bread and vegetables. I needed both but I was too proud to go in. After my father left Jaffa, he refused to take a refugee number and always thought that the dependency that UNRWA has created was a crime. I was not going to fail him.

I went into the vegetable shop. There were still no vegetables or dairy products, only the overwhelming odour of rotting food. But Samer was able to secure some bread and potatoes. He came to the car carrying three large sacks of hot steaming bread.

6 April

I can hear the sound of explosions outside. I don't know where they're coming from. I hear big crashes and thumps, followed by a loud boom. Samer called to ask if all this is close to me. I said I can hear it but I don't know how close it is to my house. Samer said he was up all night with the sound of the bombing. It was so loud it kept him from sleeping.

I am listening to Bach's *Well-tempered Clavier*. I also started the washing machine, changed the bed sheets and the towels. I cannot stand any longer to postpone these chores. I have also gone out to the garden and picked two nice bunches of flowers, some wild things that are growing on their own in my garden. Bereft of walks in the hills and flower-picking expeditions, I picked some from my garden and have put a pot in my study, a thing I've never done before. I put another in the living room. Flowers brighten up the place, make one's attitude to life so much more positive, optimistic and happy.

Control over one's world. Deciding on how one wants one's living quarters to look, what one wants to hear, how one wants to divide the day, what one wants to do in one's time, this is freedom. This is taking possession of one's life. It is like planting a garden, imposing order and attempting to beautify what is ugly, disorderly and derelict.

Penny just called. I took the telephone to the sitting room with the large window and settled for a long talk with her. She told me that she had tried to get back. She was with a large demonstration which started from Jerusalem and went to the checkpoint. At its head were an Italian band playing an oom-pah-pah with trombones and other wind instruments. The musicians were wearing funny hats. They also played partisan songs, a point that was missed by the Israeli soldiers. When they approached, the soldiers were confused. How could they possibly shoot at such a crowd? But of course they prevented them from going through the checkpoint. Penny remains behind the impregnable divide in the middle of the Jerusalem–Ramallah road, still unable to return home. She also told me that Susan, an American friend who lives in Ramallah, was able to leave Ramallah. On her way she stopped at her office next to Al Haq. She spoke to the soldiers. She told them, 'This is my office.'

'No, it's not,' one of them said. 'Now it's ours.'

She asked whether she could go in. She wanted to get her medical records.

'You wouldn't want to see what's happened in there,' he told her.

✳ ✳ ✳

Salwa's mother, who was forced to leave her house because of its proximity to Arafat's headquarters, reports that when she visited her house she found her furniture smashed and smeared with ketchup. As I heard this, I looked around me at my furniture. How would I feel if this was done to my sofa, my chairs, my table? I called Salwa. She described to me what she had been through.

'I was without water for five days,' she told me. 'I would go out under the drain to collect rainwater. The drain is too close to the ground, so I would take a pan. My back is still stiff. I would collect water to flush the toilet. The neighbours gave me a tank for cooking and drinking. Five days I almost died. And the pounding. They would smash the doors of the stores right behind my house. It felt as though their tanks were going to break into my house any minute. I had my ten-year-old niece with me. She believes this is the safest house. How could I explain to her why we were going upstairs to the neighbours? I didn't want her to be afraid. When we left the house after the curfew was lifted, she saw that the soldiers cocked their guns and she was so scared. She had seen how the soldier had shot our neighbour in the leg. She put one and one together and thought this was it. Later she told me, "I was crying from inside but couldn't let you know I was crying. I couldn't make you hear me."

'My mother is also with me and she spends the time sleeping. They entered her house. Everything was topsy-turvey. They slept on her mattress. She wouldn't let me sit on her bed and now they slept on it with their dirty boots. They broke the glass of an old antique table. They used the toilet as though they've never used a toilet. You can't imagine the state it was in. The smell, the smell, it was so awful. They threw the garbage and left it inside. All the clothes were taken out of the cupboard. When my poor mother saw this, she almost fainted. She tried to get back to my house through the fields and lost her way, either because of her state or I don't know what was wrong with her. She just lost her way. I cannot take it any more. They destroyed my office. They destroyed my mother's house, and I have to live with the constant harassment and noise here. I feel tired in my bones. The very bone of my heart rattles. I feel it. I am so deeply tired I cannot tell you. I cannot take this any more. They came to search this house. My mother said, "What are you searching for? We don't have guns. Our weapon is the justice of our cause. This you cannot find in a cupboard." She said this in Hebrew. I don't know how the words came to her head. The soldier was so furious, so furious, and started taking things apart. I told him, "If you want to search, let me help." I took out the clothes and made things a little better. But it was terrible. So terrible I cannot tell you.'

✳ ✳ ✳

The Israeli army propaganda and public relations have been very active. They claim to have found lots of weapons. They say they killed terrorists and arrested many more. That they found those who make the bombs and arrested some who were ready to carry out more bombings. They are claiming to be destroying the infrastructure of terror of the Palestinian Authority.

✳ ✳ ✳

I have just heard a rumour that the Palestinian Authority has declared the beginning of summer time. What difference does it make, winter or summer time, when the whole society has no schedules, no work, no schooling and no employment? The only time-bound activity is the lifting of the curfew. And this is determined by the Israeli army on their own time.

* * *

This is what it has come to: movement outside the house is allowed only for a few hours every four or five days. But this process of restricting our life has not started with the invasion. It began nine years ago, when the Oslo Accords were signed. First the West Bank was sealed off. Then the noose was tightened. Access to Jerusalem (which in many ways is Ramallah's lifeline) became considerably more difficult. Still we managed during this Intifada. When we went around on unpaved roads between the olive groves we called the road Tora Bora; the slightly easier and shorter detour around the Kalandia checkpoint we called Kalandiahar. Over the past nineteen months the process was accelerated. Each of the Palestinian population centres was cut off from the other. The countryside around Ramallah became inaccessible; getting out of Ramallah to go anywhere became an ordeal.

It is always remarkable how adaptable human beings are, but even for Palestinians, who have Job's patience, endurance has a limit. Now, for the past nine days, our houses have become the only centres of our lives and we have been prevented from going to our offices for work, and the children from going to school and the sick from getting medical care. An entire society has been prevented from carrying on with its life. The economy has come to a complete halt. There is talk of buffer zones that would only entrench our confinement.

But this is not all because of military necessity. The Israeli army's entry into Ramallah went practically unopposed. They knew they had not come to fight another army. They had come to abrogate, in a *de facto* if not in a *de jure* manner, the arrangement under Oslo that placed Palestinian cities, known as Area

A, under the full security control of the Palestinian Authority. The withdrawal of the territorial jurisdiction from the Palestinian Authority happened gradually. The Israeli government needed to check the tolerance of the international community. First they came to the peripheries of the town and there was no condemnation. Then they became more brazen and began to make deeper incursions and still there was no reaction. They got the message that they could occupy the whole place at no cost to their international standing. Under the terms of Oslo, they had subcontracted to the Palestinians security control over the cities. They also realized they can unilaterally withdraw this contract without risking sanctions.

The abrogation of every aspect of the Oslo Accords has been an objective of this government and it was going about realizing it. With the destruction of the Palestinian Authority, who was going to provide for the needs of the Palestinian population? As long as Israel was in effective occupation, this Authority cannot function. The Israeli army seems to want full control without the concomitant responsibilities and duties which international law places on an occupier. Israel always complained that Arabs don't recognize its existence. Now it was unwilling to recognize ours. Not only as a political entity but also as a human community. No provision was being made to provide medical care for the chronically ill or schooling for children. No one was allowed to work. The entire society was being destroyed by keeping everyone locked up behind closed doors as the members of the occupation force drove around in their tanks as recklessly as possible, destroying anything that stood in their path, cars, poles or supporting walls, acting as though the whole place was theirs, to do with it what they liked.

As we endure all this we listen to interviews with three types of Palestinians for their comments on the situation. The first is the militant. This morning's choice was someone identified as a leader of Hamas fighters in the Jenin refugee camp. His voice did not reveal great sophistication. He sounded sincere and beleaguered. He told the station that the camp was being bombarded from the air. He also said that homes were being destroyed over the heads of their inhabitants, burying them in the rubble. Ambulances are not allowed through. This man declared that he was ready to die in defence of his land.

The second type is the politician. Like all politicians the world over, he is more concerned about how he comes across. He is so good at making verbal distinctions; he has mastered the art of saying what makes no sense but sounds impressive. We have plenty of seasoned politicians who are masters of protocol and are waiting for a state to utilize their talents.

The third is the common man, the member of this beleaguered civilian society which is paying the highest price. A man on a stretcher in Bethlehem with a tube in his nose told his interviewer, 'We shall continue with the resistance and carry on with our *sumoud* until we liberate our country.' I don't know why these words coming from the mouth of this injured man brought tears to my eyes. Perhaps because no one had told him to say them. He sincerely believed in resistance. I suppose we all do. Each in his own way.

7 April

Tried to vary my routine since it was Sunday. Finished some editing work, then didn't do any other work. Read, did a little bit of gardening, prepared meals for myself and of course answered the telephone and watched news on the television. It began to settle in that this was going to take longer than I had expected.

Our friend Vera called and said that her ninety-year-old mother, who lives with her at home, fainted at night. She was very worried and tried to call an ambulance.

'Do you have tanks around you?' she was asked.

'Yes, they come and go.'

'Then we cannot come,' they said.

So she revived her mother with water and slapping. What would have happened if her mother had collapsed? She would have been completely helpless. Neither the sick nor the dead are allowed an ambulance service.

Rita's mother also became sick. 'I don't usually go out,' she told me over the telephone, 'but not to be allowed out made me very tense. I got shingles.'

An obstetrician reports that she has been instructing women over the telephone how to give birth at home. In one case the woman began to bleed. Her husband carried her and together they braved the snipers and went to hospital. 'Either we live together or die together,' the man told his wife.

8 April

Penny is back. She arrived at eleven this morning. I went to meet her at the Kalandia checkpoint. I was not allowed to approach this formidable-looking barrier now blocking the much-travelled road to Jerusalem. From a distance I saw her emerging from that other world beyond the cordon of tanks and soldiers around Ramallah. Behind her the air was embrowned with the shadows of helmeted soldiers sheltering behind newly constructed shacks covered by camouflage netting like dry seaweed, the colour of earth.

At first they would not allow her to cross. They let her through only after she convinced the soldiers that she lives in Ramallah. They told her she could enter Ramallah but would not be allowed to leave. I felt such relief when I saw her bright, happy face. We hugged. We were reunited. My solitary confinement is over.

Samer and I met Penny at the outskirts of the town, where supplies of fresh vegetables have been allowed. We saw many of our friends at the vegetable shop. Ghassan told us that his wife was abroad. 'But never mind,' he said with typical Palestinian dry humour, 'it saves on water. One shower instead of two.'

People were swarming over the vegetables. It's been days since the army has allowed fresh vegetables and dairy products into Ramallah. I noticed they were all Israeli. Palestinian growers are still prevented from selling their crop.

In Ramallah the army, with their tanks and soldiers, are stationed behind barbed wire in fixed locations. This means there was no interaction with the public, lest the soldiers discover that those they've come to terrorize are fellow human beings.

I didn't watch television last night. I read, then slept early and woke up at five-thirty. After doing some house cleaning, I showered and shaved and dressed. I wanted to stay looking tidy and follow my routine and keep things orderly and clean. It's very important for my spirits and sense of self.

But what a luxury a garden is. I realized this in 1967, when I couldn't water during the war and everything went dry and dusty – there was so much dust in the air. And now I realize what it takes to keep a good garden: nurseries, supplies, water and the right mood to do the hard labour. Much of these essential elements are not there now. To make it worse, my garden this year has been afflicted with some fungus that I was too late in treating; many plants are drooping. Today I have finally sprayed. Hopefully, things will begin to look up.

✳ ✳ ✳

There was a fire today next to the Church of the Nativity. The soldiers arrested the fire fighters who came to put it out.

Sharon made a speech to the Knesset. It was clear that he has nothing to offer. He confirmed that he was going to continue his battles (what else does he live for?). He is a man of war, committed to Israel's expansion by any means. He has added three very right-wing ministers to his government to withstand any possible American pressure. He repeated all the usual nonsense that he was ready to meet with Arab leaders anywhere, that

Arafat was a terrorist, that Israel wants to live in peace with the Palestinians. He was simply pushing the classic Likud vision of Palestinians as a disenfranchised minority in Greater Israel.

Many Israeli officials are fond of repeating that 6 million Jews died and Europe didn't lift a finger. Their message is that they are victims who can depend on no one to defend them. The lesson that was learned by them is that power, not law, is what pays in the end. Now they have the power and they accept no fetters. They feel entitled to use their army to violate the fundamental international law principle that the acquisition of territory through belligerent action is prohibited. They feel so powerful and immune that they can violate the law with impunity. What began in Israel as an admirable will to live despite all adversity has led to policies that are messianic, exclusivist, inhuman and cruel.

9 April

A beautiful April spring morning. The air is so fresh, clean and clear. The birds are singing. Even the garden, I am finding, is in a better state after I sprayed, watered and did a little bit of weeding.

And of course things are looking up now that Penny is back.

Education Minister Livnat said, at the March of the Living in Poland,[†] 'We must always be vigilant and distinguish between right and wrong.' She would do well to start with herself.

At ten in the morning in Israel a moment of silence was observed for Holocaust Day. This is always an effective exercise. What better response to a horror such as the Holocaust than silence. This is the fitting response. One survivor was interviewed on Israeli news. He said, 'My children ask me and they get nothing. They are typical of second-generation survivors. They ask but get no answers. They only get silence.'

It's the silence of those who went through horror. Words come only from those who were not there, who exploit the tragedy for their own purposes. Conduct that I am beginning to be able to understand very well.

* * *

† An annual march from the Nazi death camp in Auschwitz.

When Sharon declares that the country must defend itself, he is not speaking about the Israel of 1967 but of Israel and the territories occupied in this war. Likewise, when he announces that the country's citizens must be safe, he is referring also to Israel's citizens who are living outside their country in illegal settlements. Those outside who hear Sharon and don't know his ideological commitment do not understand this. They argue, why should Israel not have the right to defend its territory and protect its citizens? Which territory and what citizens? is the question.

* * *

I don't know why I was reminded today of my experience with the Israeli officer who served as the head of the legal unit during the last years of the Israeli military government in the West Bank before the Oslo Accords. I was then active in human rights and would go to him to argue the case of victims of his government's policies. I would describe in English, which was our common tongue, the effect on the civilian population of the collective punishment his administration was imposing, the deprivation of education, health and work. I would pour my heart out, speaking to him as a fellow human being. I would remind him that both people would one day have to live together in this small area of land and how he should be concerned about the effect of these policies on future generations of Palestinians. He would remain silent, which I would take as a good sign. The man was listening. Then suddenly I would see him baring his teeth in a cold smile. He would calmly tell me, 'I like speaking to you. It helps improve my English.'

In Israel compassion is deemed as weakness. The evil that they inflict on us, which would shock normal human beings, seems to many in Israel as nothing because it is in smaller measure than what the German Nazis inflicted upon the Jews.

✳ ✳ ✳

The news is dominated by the events at the Jenin refugee camp and in the old city of Nablus. Jenin is being called the Palestinian Massada. I don't like these allusions that harp on questionable history. The idea of a closed zone where no one knows what is taking place is bloodcurdling. Only Israel can get away with something like this and still be called a democracy.

The only real fighting has taken place in Jenin, where twenty-three Israeli soldiers were killed and six wounded. It was in Jenin that there were those who really decided to die fighting.

10 April

For the past twelve days we have been under the mercy of the Israeli army, subject to their bombing, afraid for our life. Then boom! One of our own strikes back, proving their security theory, for which we are paying, to be false. Boom. And now it is they who are subject to our threat, our bombing. They go up in flames, their bodies shatter, their buildings are damaged and destroyed. It is momentary, one single explosion, not like the incessant bombing around us, which brings about the sudden reversal of roles.

They are confused; we can see how confused they are. The gloved men wearing plastic over their shoes look for body parts. For a moment we revel in our power, the sudden reversal of our fate, our sudden, all too sudden, victory over our enemy. Then we see the old woman crying. It is no longer abstract and faceless victims, it is now harm inflicted on an individual with whom we can identify. She can be our mother, older sister or neighbour. This changes everything.

Our victory is diminished. Who of us would agree that a daughter of ours would do this for us, die on our behalf, strap her body with explosives and at a certain point turn the switch and shatter her flesh, her head, her torso, her lovely face, her hair, her delicate limbs, her brain, her feet. No, this is not how we wanted it. After the large boom is a long and unbearable silence. The victory is sour, embittering, sobering. How could it have come to this?

In that brief moment of silence, our enemy and we are joined together. Then we are both shattered and raised up into the air, together. Both remain suspended in the air before the pieces begin to fall and scatter on the ground and the victims are counted to determine whose casualties were greater, who was the winner and who the loser of this round. There are no winners and we both know it.

When a bomb explodes on the other side, everyone falls back on his or her embittering experience and imagines among the victims the interrogator who tortured, the soldier at the checkpoint who harassed, the official at the ministry who mistreated, the settler who shot, the usurper who took the land, the road builder who cut through and severed our country.

Everyone has a grievance, a sore spot in his heart and a festering memory in his head. And to counter these there are few happy memories of human encounters. Since Oslo the two sides have been back to back. The common humanity has been further violated, estranged and denied, despite the large amount of money spent on programmes to foster co-existence and common ground between the warring people.

During the first Intifada the movement of both people into the lands of the other continued to be possible. Israeli journalists reported on what was taking place in the occupied territories. The official television channel broadcast documentaries about the effect of the Israeli policies on the people and of the resistance on the soldiers. All sorts of relations developed between the people on the two sides of the divide. None of this has been possible this time. With the exceptions of a few determined Israeli journalists, it was left to the army to present to the Israeli people the reality in the occupied territories. The prohibition against travel by both sides to each other's territories meant that the demonization could continue unchallenged. Most of those going into Israel to blow themselves up would be making their first trip to that part of the land. It's easier to kill and harass demons than human beings.

* * *

The situation in Jenin continues to be uppermost in my mind. I don't know what was the army's plan for the camp. I know what happened at Amari refugee camp near Ramallah during the previous invasion. The soldiers used the tactic of burrowing in the camp like you would do into a rabbit hole. Rather than go from house to house along the street and risk getting shot, they went into one house and opened (by explosion or drill or hammer) a hole in the wall and from there they got to the next house. Fluorescent arrows pointed to the soldiers coming behind which way to go. They seem to have had no consciousness that they were entering human dwellings; they were playing a game without regard to the presence of humans, revealing utter disrespect for their life and property.

One woman whose kitchen had just been renovated begged the soldiers not to destroy her new fridge. Another in Aida camp near Bethlehem was shot and the soldiers watched as she bled to death, refusing to allow the ambulance to get to her. Israel's Channel 2 footage of this event made something of an uproar among Israeli society, which was shocked by its own soldiers' callousness.

Were the commanders of the Israeli army exploring the limits of what their soldiers would be able to tolerate in preparation for worse deeds yet to come?

* * *

I began to worry when I heard the news that the chief of staff, Shaul Mofaz, himself was taking over command of the operation in the Jenin camp. How far would this hawkish man go to accomplish a 'victory' before his term as chief of staff ended?

Samer's advice was sought by his friends in Nablus before it was invaded. He was called in his capacity as someone who had experienced the ordeal of having soldiers in his house. But after the invasion, his Nablus friends called to assure him that what he endured was nothing compared to what they were experiencing. It's never a consolation when your friends have suffered more.

All morning we have been hearing explosions. Samer reports that there are tanks down in the valley overlooking his house (where I used to go for walks) and they are shelling anything that moves. I wonder who could be there. We used to see gazelles picking their graceful way up the terraced hills.

The news from Jenin is of continuous bombardment from helicopter gunships. One sociology professor interviewed by the BBC said they were killing the fighters rather than taking them prisoners and they were destroying the camp. The human imagination closes off and prevents the attempt to fathom and identify with catastrophe. I realized this as I listened to descriptions of the fighting in Jenin.

As I write I can hear such sustained shooting outside. As

though these soldiers are making a point, expressing their anger and revenge on whoever or whatever they can target.

* * *

On the diplomatic front some hopeful signs and calls even by the US for international peacekeepers and for Israel to withdraw. Alas, the withdrawal being called for is from the latest reoccupation. Even after they withdraw, our country will remain occupied.

There has not been any garbage collection since 30 March. What pests and health hazards will this lead to? Many areas of Ramallah are without a sewerage system. The sewers will soon begin to overflow. We await Colin Powell's arrival to solve these mundane problems.

* * *

For exercise Penny and I march around in the house to the tune of some fast-tempo music. As I pass the big draped French window of the sitting room after every circuit I can see the hazy outline of the hills to the south-east with the humps of green trees and the houses across from mine with the red tiles. The hills seem so distant, as though they don't belong to me and I no longer have the right to walk in them. The houses look so quiet and lifeless, as though they have been deserted.

This is an entirely new use of the house. Now with Penny back, the confinement is easier to endure. We have elaborate dinners with soft music. During the day we are both very busy with our own work. Penny has been preparing a report on the inhabitants of the Jenin camp to counter the impression that the refugee camp is a military garrison. We take turns answering the telephone.

My elderly secretary called, she's been sick at home. 'I heard a lot of shooting,' she said. 'These snipers on the Casablanca Hotel next to our house keep on shooting all the time. I don't know what they're shooting at unless it's the birds. When my sister lets Lucky, the dog, out she tells him, "Go and come back quickly." She stays waiting by the door and it is as though he understands. He comes back quickly into the house.'

✳ ✳ ✳

The gorgeous spring is here with its wonderful fruits and vegetables. How are the farmers managing? Those who can get to their fields to pick their crop cannot bring it to the market. Who will compensate them? What will this do to their simple economy? I keep thinking of the spring walks we are missing. Penny and I yearn to be able to go out to a café or the movies or to see friends. It must be hell for people cooped up in small houses with large families. And then we have to hear how all this is necessary so that the Israeli people can live normal lives and go out to cafés and on to the streets. What is it all for but to pursue an expansionist colonialist policy? This is what we, both Palestinians and Israelis, are suffering for.

11 April

Kofi Annan's description of the humanitarian situation as intolerable was on the mark. Every morning brings more devastating news of yet more inhumanity, senseless, vindictive, brutal destructive action on the part of the Israeli army. I just spoke to Nabeel. He asked me if I can go out to the garden. He said he couldn't. He has snipers around his house. They have said anyone seen outside will be shot. One woman was hanging her washing when they shot her. He believes she died. Why shoot a woman hanging her washing? What subversive activity could this be? How could a soldier have it in him to do something like this?

The army have been conducting house to house searches. In his street they have gone into the building where my cousin used to live. They blew up every door of every single empty apartment. These were the sounds we were hearing yesterday. In all the building they found only one couple, a man and his Swedish wife. They arrested him and have presumably taken him to the nearby Ofer camp. The Israeli human rights organization B'tselem has said a soldier who is stationed there called them and reported that the detainees were being tortured.

'I don't understand why they took him,' Nabeel told me. 'He is such a mild man. He has no political involvement.'

When Nabeel asked why would they want him, I knew he was thinking of himself. If this mild man who was uninvolved in politics could be arrested, why couldn't he?

The army has also been breaking into governmental and non-governmental organizations, destroying the offices and helping themselves to computer hard disks and records. As Nabeel put it, 'They are destroying institutional memory built over many years of hard work.'

The more I hear of this, the more I worry about my law office. Our files begin in 1949. What if they should destroy them or burn up the office?

I just heard the noise of a large vehicle outside my window. I thought that it could be a tank. Then voices of people. Have the army decided to search our house? I looked out of the window. Penny came running to say, 'It's a garbage truck.' A garbage truck, great news. Excited, I left the house and walked to the garden to congratulate them. I asked one of the men (he was short and pudgy and looked proud of himself to be on the street when everyone else was locked inside), 'Did you coordinate this with the army?'

'What?' he asked, as if I were mad. 'The Cross is with us. Who would dare go out alone in this time? He'd get shot.'

And indeed I looked behind the garbage truck and saw the four-wheel-drive white vehicle with the Red Cross insignia and flag driven by a proud Swiss female delegate of the international organization, now an honorary member of our town's garbage collectors.

***

There is news that Israeli army bulldozers have demolished homes over the heads of their inhabitants in the Jenin camp. If true, then this is a new escalation, a further demonstration of Israel's position that the Palestinians are not human beings. So many of the inhabitants of the camp have been forced out to the mosques and the open fields. They number 4,000. In Israel's eyes they are all terrorists who deserve no shelter or relief. When I heard this and thought about it, I realized that the Israeli propaganda has not changed. In the eyes of the extremists, no Palestinian society with rights exists. We are all a bunch of terrorists whom it is legitimate for Israel to treat as befits terrorists. We do not deserve to have institutions. We have no right to our achievements, no right to have records for the population, nothing that belongs to us has sanctity, we don't even have the right to our own home. Who will protect us against the ravages of the Israeli army? This is why we can be placed under weeks of twenty-four-hour curfew, as we wait in our homes for the brutal Israeli army to come to search, vandalize and arrest. It is legitimate to destroy our homes, cars and offices. Destroy our institutions and our economy and leave us without a future. Because, in the view of Sharon and his supporters (now a majority in Israel, according to the polls), we have no right to be here. This land does not belong to us. It belongs to the Jews and must be settled only by them. We must either accept to live under their rule on their own terms or leave.

When all this is over, will Israel be forced to admit guilt and pay compensation? Will it make amends in words and deeds? Judging from previous experiences, Israel will admit to no wrongdoing. It will simply claim that all this was necessary, all an act of war. All done to protect the Israeli people. When has Israel ever admitted or paid for any of its wrongdoings?

* * *

This morning Rita, who runs the Institute of Community and Public Health at Birzeit University, called.

'How are you?' I asked.

'Terrible,' she answered in a low, sad voice. 'They are in Birzeit. They are near my office. They have not entered yet, but I am burning from inside. I am so worried they will go in and destroy all my files, my work, my computers. It's my life's work. What do you think I can do? They went into the ophthalmic clinic of Medical Relief and destroyed all the big expensive machines and took away the patients' records. Now they even have our eye records. What about your office, have they entered it yet?'

'It has a big lock. They have not been able to open it,' I said.

'The Medical Relief Loan Centre also had strong locks. When the lock would not open, they demolished the whole wall and vandalized the place.'

I tried to think of what could be done. I thought of the Red Cross. But they were busy escorting garbage trucks.

'Nothing can be done,' I had to confess to Rita. 'Nothing at all.'

* * *

We are alone with our private worries about our property, homes, offices, the places in which we invested years and years of our lives.

What is bewildering is how systematic the destruction has been and how inhuman and senseless. In 1996 a group of volunteers established the Thalassemia Patients' Friends Society. This is an inherited and lethal Mediterranean anaemia that afflicts about 3 per cent of new-born babies annually in Palestine. It leaves its patients with an average life expectancy of fifteen years. The society aims at spreading awareness of the disease and working towards its elimination in Palestine. Its offices were not in an area of fighting. Still the Israeli army broke the external door, then a wall which divides the office from the inner stairwell. Once inside, the army caused extensive damage, the medical and office equipment was strewn on the floor and broken. Medical infusion pumps used by patients to take their life-saving medication were torn apart and medication vials were broken and thrown on the floor. The three computers in the office were destroyed, with the hard disks removed. Two office desks were broken, as were the TV, VCR and scanner. The shelves were pulled down and patients' files and records were scattered across the office. Money was also taken from donation boxes. A brand-new computer and new printer, both donations to the society, were stolen. How does the vandalism of such an office help protect Israelis?

✷ ✷ ✷

On television I saw a soldier in a tank driving out of Ramallah, raising his two fingers and brandishing the V-sign as he smiled with strong white teeth and an amiable round face. What victory? This is not the sort of fighting that any decent soldier could be proud of, driving in a tank down lanes between people's homes, shooting at a woman hanging the laundry on her balcony, killing civilians and destroying private homes and institutions. He should be hiding his face in shame.

✳ ✳ ✳

The town was dark and grim, as though a cloud hung over it, though the weather was clear and bright. Was it the dust or was the gloom in our soul?

It's almost not worth it. I'm just back from one of those 'prison furloughs'. In Israeli prisons they call them *fora*, an Arabic word that denotes overflow. It is as though during these few hours which we come to hear about without prior notice, we brim out of our houses into the public spaces that have not been closed off by the Israeli army and then, a few hours later, return to our homes. On this most recent *fora* I went with my brother. Every shop was full. People were pushing through the congested aisles, inquiring after each other, kissing and exchanging news and offering congratulations on being safe. This was causing obstruction. But the greatest annoyance was the feeling that the life of the society has been reduced to buying and hoarding enough food to last during our imprisonment. All that people do is shop, cook, eat and wait for the next occasion when curfew is lifted to shop again. No income, no work, no pleasure.

Next time curfew is lifted I don't want to shop. I want to walk around like a normal human being, visit people, do something more sociable and fun.

✳ ✳ ✳

I don't dare go to my office. I am afraid that if I succeed in opening the door that has been bent I would not be able to close it again. And then there would be no time to bring a blacksmith to get the door to close again. My partner is superstitious. He does not want me to touch the door lest our luck with the soldiers turns.

But to think that for two weeks now I have not been able to go in and see if there is anything urgent, read the faxes and catch up with the life of my profession and business. A colleague of mine has his law office in the same building as Al Haq. It is now part of the new army post.

✳ ✳ ✳

During my excursion I visited the house of a school headmistress which the army had invaded. The woman and her husband were staying with her mother. They have a small house right by the street on which I live. In their front garden the roses were in bloom: white, red and mauve. Further towards the wall wild flowers, red poppies and yellow mustard seed, were in bloom. The soldiers entered through this colourful garden, placed a bomb and exploded the door of the glass veranda. They then entered the cosy room with the couch draped with a floral material, next to which was the small reading lamp with the yellow shade. The bomb made two holes in this room, one in the floor in front of the couch and the other in the stone wall behind it. Then they proceeded to blast the main door of the house. Once inside, they wreaked havoc on the place, removing all the clothes from the wardrobes and destroying the television and the furniture. I visited the woman after she had discovered what had been done to her house. She told me, 'What can I say when I know that elsewhere there are families buried alive under the rubble? I can only say thank God. Material possessions can be replaced.'

After our visit Samer remembered that he needed oranges and was turning to go into another of those jammed streets when I felt I could not take it any more. I felt my whole body jittery and anxious. I said no. I didn't want to see any more shops. He drove Penny and me to my mother's for lunch. But he did not return for lunch. I found myself fretting. What could have happened to him? I was so anxious. I told myself, but what could happen? The traffic is so bad, could he have had an accident? I knew I was being unreasonable. One can drive on only a few streets. What could happen in such short distances and he is a good driver in a big car? But then why has he not come back? What could be wrong?

Then, when Penny and I left Mother I felt so sad to leave her alone. She seemed so bored. Perhaps I could encourage her to come down just for a walk around the block, and yet it is not safe, maybe I shouldn't. I was not sure what was right. I was not feeling myself. I wanted to be back home. I didn't want to be out any more. I am more anxious and unhappy than I had realized.

✳✳✳

The open fields behind my house are so green with the April rain. The red poppies are in abundance. I took a short walk in my neighbourhood before getting locked up again. There was a small boy with his father in the field behind my house picking flowers. He had a beautiful red bunch of poppies. He waved them at me. I smiled at him. He seemed so happy. None of us could linger in the beautiful fields. The afternoon was long but we had to be home. Curfew was about to be imposed again.

12 April

According to the BBC, there are over 4,000 Palestinian detainees. Once again, blindfolded, shirtless Palestinians can be seen from bus windows being taken to an unknown destination, treated like animals and possibly tortured.

No wonder the emotions of the first Intifada are returning, the anger at the Israelis, at their violence and brutality, at their arrogant army. How did this society in such a short time produce such a number of obdurate and insular people? And the number of propagandists, thinkers and writers who are willing to repeat such propaganda as: let the Palestinians convince us that they want peace, there can be no peace as long as the terrorist Arafat is there, in Camp David we offered them more than any other country in history. I know some of these people. How can they allow themselves to believe that they are doing a legitimate national service by repeating this propaganda to foreign journalists?

Am I failing in my national, patriotic duty by remaining silent, refusing to be interviewed, become a spokesman and repeat slogans? But I don't want to. I don't think a writer owes a duty to his country to become a propagandist and a pamphleteer even under conditions as difficult as ours.

With the passing of every day I feel angrier because I am restricted from walking, from going places in my car, from taking breaks away from the house, from going on with my life, going to my office, seeing my nephew and niece, going out for dinner or to see a film. My car battery has died from non-use.

* * *

I've just heard that Rita's office is safe. They didn't go in. She contacted everyone in the world. Did this make a difference? I doubt it. Should I contact people I know in Israel for the army to stay away from my office? But I don't want to ask anyone for a favour. Yet if my office is ransacked, I would go mad. I don't know what to do.

Samer says he eats only one meal a day. In the evening he cannot eat. 'I'm too nervous,' he told me. 'Last night the tanks were parked at the corner of my street. We were in a state for hours.'

'Why?' I asked. 'They have already been to your house. They will not come again.'

'They came three times to some houses,' he told me.

* * *

A series of images on the BBC from the Jenin refugee camp: a woman in a wheelchair alone in a dirt lane in need of help, people crying, people wounded and no ambulances allowed, houses demolished.

The journalists who captured these images on camera could not venture further. The camp remains closed to all, including humanitarian organizations, even when the fighting has ended. The electricity and water have been cut for over a week now. How are the people inside managing? No food or medical services have been allowed. While their country is pursuing such inhuman policies, some Israeli intellectuals offer themselves as apologists for the ugly deeds of their country.

It is just infuriating to listen to Israeli spokespeople. They repeat the word terror a million times. We the Palestinians are terrorists and therefore anything they do to us is legitimate. We are treated as *homo sacer* – to whom the laws of the rest of humanity do not apply. We deserve the suffering inflicted on us because we refused to accept their generous offer at Camp David to be confined to Bantustans where we could run our own domestic affairs while we see the rest of our country enjoyed by the illegal settlers. But the worst offence of all is to have to listen to the claim that the Israeli army is among the most moral and has done all it could to avoid civilian casualties.

There is something pornographic about Sharon's repetition of the word terrorist in his full-mouthed manner. Isn't pornography the denigration of the human being into a mere object, a mere body, and a toy to which things can be done? So with the Palestinians, who are now dubbed terrorists. They can be killed, disposed of like flies by the army's big machines without second thought. Then it is simply announced, 'We killed two more terrorists.' I find that I cannot stand any more to hear the word.

I'm getting angry and I don't want to be angry. I also don't want to be the subject of pity. I don't want to be determined by the Israeli army or by Palestinian politicians. I know this process from before, the turning of every Palestinian into a terrorist and therefore fair game. I can imagine that when they came to the headmistress's house they did not see it as the house of a decent family but the abandoned house of a terrorist that deserves to be destroyed. It is the propaganda and programming that blunt their ability to have empathy with other humans and turn them into racists.

And none of this has changed over the years. Oslo was not a breakthrough; it was a hiatus. It kept the Israeli army at bay for a few years. But no element of the conflict was resolved. The building of the settlements continued and neither side showed any signs of coming to terms with the past.

The more the day progresses the more my feelings of fear, hate and frustration echo those of the first Intifada. The Israeli army is interested not only in controlling my life but also in claiming my mind, emotions and attitudes: I am the person who wants Israeli women and children and babies to die. I do not appreciate life and freedom. And as an intellectual, I am a disappointment because I am blinded by hatred and intimidated by the extremists. Colonial rule is not just a set of laws and regulations, but assumptions and attitudes and attempts at capturing the mind and heart of the colonized. Of course I know this. For many years I lived through and struggled against it. But I thought that I had overcome it. My angry response to what is taking place now makes me wonder.

✳ ✳ ✳

In between our frantic shopping today we stopped at Samer's office to get a document that he needed. His office is in a tall building within shooting range of the Israeli settlement of Psagot. But it has not been shelled. It was saved because of the presence there of the Swiss and Canadian representative offices to the Palestinian Authority. We took the lift up to the top floor. Everything was so orderly. The guard had watered the plants and saved them from dying. We walked through impressive wooden doors to the empty offices of Samer's secretaries and assistants, the meeting room and the archives. The fax machine had a large stack of unread messages. For two weeks now no one has answered the telephone or responded to clients or contracted business. Like all of the rest of the life of this society, everything has been halted. The largest insurance company in the country has been brought to a complete standstill. For two weeks now the entire society has been deprived of two weeks of life.

* * *

Now it's time to listen to the news again. Sharon and Powell are holding a joint press conference.

How painful it is to have to listen to the sanctimonious tone of American diplomats who, when speaking about foreign affairs, sound like priests. It is, I suppose, the annoyance of someone under the rubble who has to tolerate all the talk of uncaring relief workers who ramble on when he knows what needs to be done. Why don't they simply remove the beam over his chest and allow him once again to breathe?

These diplomatic affairs are like playing charades. You have to guess at the script from their silent gestures and body language, and they are all such good actors that they keep straight faces. Sharon welcomed Powell to Jerusalem, 'the united capital of the Jewish people'. Powell, we thought, was taken aback. He said the usual spiel about appreciating his 'good friend Sharon' and the constructive talks they had had. Why should intelligent humans who have other, better things to do have to listen to this? I'm too angry, bored and distressed to play games.

There is breaking news: another Palestinian bombing. The cries of an old woman screaming in shock can be heard. Then they get the usual suspects to exploit the tragedy: the suave, handsome Israeli spokesman with an English accent. I want to scream, This is not just a public relations exercise. The Israelis are being hit and have casualties and our life has been brought to a standstill. We are killing each other. We have to stop. This is what is important, not what the outside world thinks.

13 April

There seems to be no end to it. Yet another curfew day. It's already over two weeks. With the exception of a few hours, a whole society has been under a twenty-four-hour curfew for two weeks. No provisions have been made for the risk groups: the diabetics who need insulin shots or those with kidney failure who need dialysis, or children who need inoculations. It is murderous.

The facts are coming out. In Nablus a family of eight, including three children, was buried under the rubble of a house the Israelis demolished over its inhabitants. In Jenin the high court has ruled against the army burying the dead. But still it is not clear how many died and whether the army buried them in mass graves.

A group of women who had fled were interviewed.

'Have you seen?' they were asked.

'Yes, we have,' they answered.

'You saw with your own eyes?'

I don't know if these women are telling the truth. I know they are twice refugees now. How often have I seen this image of Palestinian women, their traditional dress wrapped over bundles of flesh, carrying goods wrapped in cloth on their heads, saying they've had no water and have been unable to wash, with the image of their demolished homes behind them. I looked at the blank faces of the soldiers in the tank parked next to these wretched women; they are beginning to look the picture of white supremacists.

* * *

The Palestinian leaders trapped in the Muqata look haggard. Their garbage is piling up in their offices; they have scarcity of water and intermittent electricity. They now have long beards. And Israel is still blaming Arafat for not taking care of the 'terror'. Among the rubble the foreign minister of Egypt steps in, kisses and holds hands over hand. I watch this show. There was something admirable about Arafat. He is the only Arab leader who does not go for luxuries. He could have betrayed his people and accepted the offer made at Camp David and ended up the head of a state of a sort. To his credit, he didn't. And yet why do I think that the regime he has developed looks like the ruling regimes of the Arab world? It must be because, watching these gestures, we the wretched public are expected to feel proud of the performance of our leadership because they are still able to carry on with the diplomatic game (which my mother says is more like a game of musical chairs) when none of our daily needs have been provided for.

As usual it falls upon civil society (which the PA fought so viciously when it had the power) to prepare fact sheets and meet with Powell, as they are doing today to brief him on the assessment of damage. Where are the Palestinian ministers, the regime's executive, and what have they done to assess the damage and speak about it to the world? The important thing is to attend meetings at the top. Symbolism has killed us throughout the decades and brought our society to ruin. We remain dependent on outside aid rather than building our own society and taking responsibility for ourselves.

***

I have just read Islah's account over the Internet of the death of Jad, her son's friend. She asks, 'Who was it who gave arms to this young man? How could he have the heart to leave him out in the street to face Israeli tanks without protection or shelter? Would this officer be held to account for his criminal negligence, his failure to carry out his duties towards those under his care?'

I pace around the house and think of these matters. It is a good thing that I have a large house.

14 April

These past fourteen days of war have reached a crescendo in the war crimes in Jenin and the continued siege of some 200 people trapped in the Church of the Nativity in Bethlehem. The Israeli army is preventing the media from entering Jenin camp. But then the smell of rotting flesh cannot be kept back. It slowly permeates, revealing what the government was determined to conceal. It's as though Ariel Sharon will not depart this world until this lovely land has been drenched with the stench of death.

For years he has been sowing the seeds of hatred and conflict through his unremitting work at settling Israelis on Palestinian land. He has had a following, but it was a minority among the Israeli public. The fear the Palestinian bombers engendered among Israelis brought him success. His countrymen support his policy of force and terror against the Palestinians. Unless the link is made between the injustice and the cruelty of the policy of planting strangers in the land of others and the violence it inevitably breeds, our region will continue to be mired in war, violence and brutality. If only the Israelis would ask themselves what they would have done if they were forced to endure what we are enduring.

* * *

This occupation began at the end of March. Most salaried people had not been paid their salary. They had already spent last month's salary and were left with nothing. A friend of mine told me he only has fifty shekels left. During the last lifting of curfew he used them to buy cigarettes and bread. All week he lived on *zait* and *zaitar* (oil and thyme) and olives. At least he has the appetite to eat. Another friend of mine told me about Jamil, a colleague of his who, he said, has become so gaunt and frail. For days he has been unable to put anything in his mouth. He lives across from a butchery. When the electricity went out, all the meat rotted. The stench was horrible; it hung in the air. A few days later his neighbour's sister died. She could not be buried. When he went to pay his respects the fetid odour of her decomposing flesh filled the house. Now he can no longer eat.

Not only are people prevented from going to work, they must remain at home and suffer the nerve-racking noise of the various explosions and sporadic shooting taking place the whole day and most of the night. My mother says they stop only at mealtimes. As they listen, they can't help wondering: was this my shop or office or clinic that has been bombed and the door exploded and the contents smashed? Sometimes the tank would knock down an electric pole and the electricity would be cut from an entire neighbourhood. During the last lifting of curfew we passed a house which had no electricity. Samer said the owner recognizes the tank that persists in carrying out the damage. He told him, 'It's tank number 11. I know it well. Every time I see it passing I wait for the damage it is going to do. It either knocks down a telephone pole or an electricity pylon or a wall. Maybe he's a new driver.'

Every office, shop, lab, clinic or residence that for any reason was empty ran the risk of bombardment, forced entry and looting by the Israeli army. This has been taking place long after the army had assumed full control of the city and was meeting with absolutely no resistance.

And every night people wait. Would this be the night when the army would force its way into my house to search it, causing havoc and destruction to my belongings and driving fear into the hearts of my family? A whole nation without exercise or a haircut, without work for a whole month, sits at home subject to these unnatural tensions, living at the mercy of soldiers instructed by their superiors to harass the population they have occupied. The physical occupation of the Palestinian territories has been accomplished; now the psychological warfare against the very spirit of the people is proceeding.

❋ ❋ ❋

When the curfew was lifted four days ago, Shamieh, the mechanic, came to recharge my car battery. He described to me what happened when the soldiers came to search his house.

'They came twice,' he said. 'The first time they were very polite. They looked around briefly and went out. They were wonderful. But the second time. Oh, the second time it was so terrible. I don't wish it on anyone. For six hours they kept us out of the house and took it apart.

'They arrived in two tanks and a personnel carrier. They surprised us. My brother who lives in the downstairs apartment appeared at the door, the sten gun in his neck. They grabbed me by the neck and threw me outside. I told the soldier take it easy. "*Sheket*," he yelled at me. They took all of us out. The neighbour called my sister and she told her, "I can see them from my window. They are emptying your brother's house. One of them is throwing goods down from the window upstairs into the bag of another soldier standing in the garden." They took many things: my mother's old Palestinian passport, the one with the three languages, Hebrew, English and Arabic. They took the laissez-passer of my wife and our original birth certificates. They took perfume bottles. My son works with mobile phones; they took the Orange card and some brand-new phones in their boxes. They also broke the presents. We are preparing for when he gets married. They are still in their boxes; they threw them on the floor and broke them. I had some money in the *hawieh* [identity card]. There was with them a tall blond guy, their commander, an *ajnabi* [foreigner]. He saw the money and he handed it over to me. I had mentioned to him that I was keeping gold in the house. He said, "don't worry, nothing will be lost." Later I saw that they had opened the box where I hid the gold and threw the contents over the pile of our clothes. None of it had been taken. I didn't want to complain about the thievery because I heard that someone else complained and they arrested her children for six days. But of course they ended up taking my sons anyway.'

'My sons were treated like doormats', Shamieh told me. 'Are you Jihad Islami or Hamas? Tell me now. Tell me,' the soldier bellowed at them. They were neither. The soldier had checked their identity cards and knew they couldn't be either, they are Christian Palestinians. But this minor detail did not matter. The soldier sees all Palestinians as one.

When the soldiers entered the house of Ramzi, a physicist by training who works at Birzeit University, the officer asked him in a threatening voice, 'Where are the guns?' He answered in his gentle, logical manner, 'Right here in your hand.'

Last night the army knocked at the door of an old woman of eighty. When she opened and saw the soldiers with their wide-brimmed camouflage hats like crushed cook's hats and black paint smeared on their cheeks, all pointing their guns at her, she fainted. The officer entering the house was annoyed. He began to slap her face in an attempt to awaken her, saying, 'We are human. Human beings just like you.' She woke up, took one look at the soldiers and fainted again.

15 April

I was joking when I told a friend that we should be paid for being the players in this soap opera that the whole Arab world is watching. And tonight I was vindicated. Saudi television initiated a campaign to collect aid for Palestinians. Piles of jewellery were on display on a large table. Next to it was a table full of money which was being counted by four people. And numerous contributions were being promised through the fax, including four mules, land and a kidney 'or any other part of the body needed by a Palestinian'. I was surprised that no one offered us time to compensate for the weeks we lost of our lives.

It is almost spiteful of nature that this spring should be the loveliest. With the last heavy rains of April, the flowers and greenery have been abundant. I can see the overflow in the seams of the valley, by the side of the road. But the valley itself is out of bounds. Why has nature chosen this of all years, the spring of our confinement in the house, to be so lush and beautiful?

In response to an expansionist warrior nation at one's doorstep, what does one do? Life is too short and I realize my time in it may end before this problem is resolved. I cannot postpone living until it is over. This occupation has become a fact of life, one of those afflictions one has to learn to endure and live with while fighting and working to bring it to an end.

Yet despite the confinement and difficulties of life here,

Penny and I are not thinking of leaving. Our place is here. Mother says she wants to stay to see the end of this story. It is fortunate that she is fortified by her interest in narrative.

I'm getting better at managing under crisis and enduring difficult conditions. I don't exhaust and consume myself by strong emotions. I've learned how to create small spaces of my own in which to live. I'm continuing to exercise for half an hour by vigorously walking around the courtyard with appropriate music blasting. Today it was Shostakovich quintets.

* * *

Penny has been pointing out my use of the pronoun 'they' to refer to everything Israeli: the army, the government, the people. This is exactly what the right-wing government in Israel encourages, that we come to see Israel as one demonic, faceless mass of soldiers who just spurt out orders, shoot and bomb and perpetrate atrocities and inhuman actions to revenge their dead and atone for the horror their society experienced at the hands of the Palestinian bombers. Fortunately several Israeli friends have been calling to ask about us. Some of them are involved in oppositional political action against the occupation, distributing relief products and going on demonstrations. None of them is politically involved. They are thrust in this and are forced to act political. This region leaves one with no choice. Eva, an old Israeli friend, kept saying how ashamed she was. What use to me is her feeling of shame? I remember early on in the Intifada I was crossing the Kalandia checkpoint. It was hot and the soldiers were behaving in a beastly manner. As I trudged along on the dirt road that we were forced to take, I saw a group of elderly

Israeli women carrying placards walking back and forth among the miserable crowds expressing their solidarity with our suffering. I remember feeling unmoved by their gesture. We don't need spectators to witness our suffering and tell us they feel with us. We need help to put a stop to it.

∗ ∗ ∗

Just saw more pictures of the destruction in Jenin. One was the inevitable picture of an old woman with the traditional dress in floral patterns and a white headscarf waving both her hands in the air, pointing to the destruction, calling through the camera on the world, 'See what they've done to us.' She pointed at a destroyed house, then stooped as though to put her head under. 'They demolished this house over our heads,' she cried.

The horror of demolishing a home on those inside it. And refusing cries of help.

It was reported that one man was discovered still alive under the rubble in the Jenin camp. He was crying, 'Help me, help me.' There will always be someone left to tell the story. The Israeli army can never hope to destroy a whole community and hide the evidence. Someone will be left alive to tell the world what was done.

∗ ∗ ∗

The soldiers searched the house of a friend. They did not behave badly. But as they were leaving he could not help cursing them. They heard him.

'Where is your car?' they asked him.

'In the garage,' he answered.

'Take it out and park it on the street,' they ordered.

He did.

When they went out they drove their tank over it, turning it into a mass of mangled metal.

✳ ✳ ✳

Once again Susan, who has now returned to Ramallah, went over to the soldiers stationed in her office to ask their permission to take some papers out of her office. She must have caused them to experience cognitive dissonance. She turned her long, elegant body gracefully, her shoulders held back, her spine straight, over which rested her beautiful head with the straight nose and blue eyes. She moved her head back and put forward her left foot like a ballet dancer. They looked at her. What could such a beautiful woman be doing here among the terrorists?

✳ ✳ ✳

Our friend, Rema, along with businessmen and a lawyer, met with Powell and briefed him about the extensive damage the army did to local institutions. They asked him to visit the Jenin camp. They told him, 'As we sit here today, lives could be saved if the blockade around the camp is lifted.' The secretary of state of the greatest power could not prevail on his country's ally to allow humanitarian relief through that could save human life.

17 April

There were lots of sounds of explosions last night. I thought they were not real bombs, only sound bombs. 'No,' Penny said, looking out of the window, 'I can see sparks in the sky.'

This morning I learned that what we heard were fireworks from the settlements of Psagot and Givat Ze'ev, to the east and south-west of Ramallah, in celebration of Israel's independence day.

Many of the people of Ramallah were able to watch the sky from their windows and see it lit up. Some could also see the bonfire blazing in the towering settlement of Psagot, lighting the cannons pointing their barrels menacingly at their homes.

When Rabin was alive he mentioned Psagot as one of the settlements which had to be evacuated. Why do we need a Jewish neighbourhood next to Ramallah, he said publicly. The right wing felt threatened and murdered the prime minister, who was willing to make certain compromises for peace. He went. The settlement stayed. Then the right wing did even better. They elected a prime minister who was willing to jeopardize the future of their country in his determination to preserve all the settlements. Through him they were able to establish the link between the life of the country and the life of the settlements. If one goes the other goes. No peace with compromise.

* * *

The woman in Jenin, hands flaring up in the air, cried out, 'Jarrafo el shuhada bil jaraafat' (They scooped the martyrs with the bulldozers). She was repeating the same sentence over and over. She was repeating it to herself because she was finding it difficult to accept. How could it be that her son or husband or grandson be scooped like garbage, pushed with the sharp metal mouth of a bulldozer, dumped in a ditch like dirt? She was repeating it in order for her to come to terms with her own tragedy. She was in shock. She was saying what she herself found incredible and impossible to believe. Her use of the word *shuhada* (martyrs) to refer to her son or husband was in order to impress the fact on the public. It was as though what is precious and holy to everyone is being desecrated. It was not only her loss but a public loss and so listen, O public, to what they have done, they have scooped the martyrs with the bulldozers. It is not her loss alone, not her shame, but the shame of all of us, our disgrace, our defeat.

Next to her were women throwing the earth up in the air with their fingers in disbelief that their loved ones were buried alive in it.

✳ ✳ ✳

At the independence day celebration in the house of the Israeli president there was a ceremony honouring the best twenty soldiers. Mofaz, the chief of staff, was smiling as he had not done for a long time. He was the commander of a victorious army which had carried out atrocities against Palestinians. They had invited fighters from their various wars. This is how they distinguish themselves, with wars and fighting. They all drank champagne.

Israel is a state built around the army. The citizens' image of their army and the reality are far apart. If they would listen I could tell them: their army is not pure, it is murderous; it is not disciplined, it has looters; it is not above politics, it is fighting the battle of the settlers.

This spring every child in Israeli schools is required to write his or her first letter to a soldier. The children in the settlement schools wrote asking the soldiers 'to kill as many Arabs as possible'. One asked, 'For me, kill at least ten.' Another made an even simpler suggestion: 'Ignore the laws and spray them.' The spokeswoman for the settlers praised these expressions as 'healthy hatred'. She saw the suggestion to ignore the Israeli law as a healthy, practical and mature approach.

To cheer up my nephew I told him that Easter is coming and we will have a big egg hunt this year in our garden. In a low voice, as though he still felt the presence of the Israeli soldiers in his house, he asked, 'Will the Jews let us?' And my heart shattered.

18 April

When the curfew lifted today I stood out and looked at the inaccessible hills. I had never seen them so remote before, as areas of danger and peril. For the first time I could understand how my forefathers must have considered them: places where bandits hide. I was fortunate to have had a short period of respite when I was able to explore them without fear in this land of perpetual war.

The sky had white, fast-moving clouds that cast their shadow on the hills. When they slid away the terrace rocks looked whiter than usual, not their usual grey. I wondered why this was so. Was it the quality of the spring light, filtered through the clouds, or because of the contrast with the green grass below the olive trees and the new shrubs? This is the only time of year that these hills have so much greenery. It does not last long.

✳ ✳ ✳

Our neighbours who live in the elaborate house stopped by. I said hello. They told me that they were leaving for Amman and wanted me to keep the key to their house, in case the soldiers came. I said, what if the soldiers got to their house and exploded the door before I saw them?

'I don't care,' said the woman. 'We're bored. We've had enough. I put away a few things. Let them come. We want to have a few good days in Amman.'

'What about the school for the children?'

'School? What school? It's unlikely schools will open again this year.'

'The army said it would leave by Sunday.'

'Oh, yes? They said they have left Jenin and they just came back.'

'How will you get out?'

'We'll find a way.'

20 April

It was heartbreaking to see a man climb up a mound of rubble, put his head in the hole left by a beam that had settled over the mound and call out for some relative whom he hopes may yet be alive underneath. To think that there may have been survivors and the Israeli army would not allow relief workers until enough time had passed when there was no possibility that any would be alive. Or to see a woman in a wheelchair with nowhere to go. Or a family sitting around an injured elderly man who was dying for lack of medical attention and the refusal to allow an ambulance through to take him to hospital. With few exceptions the Israeli public has remained quiet throughout. Not even public rumblings could be heard against the army's inhumanity.

Uri Avneri, the veteran Israeli peace activist, described what happened in Jenin as a legend upon which dreams are built, informing and defining (and perhaps warping) the consciousness of the emerging Palestinian nation state.

We've had enough catastrophes; we don't need more to equip us with the necessary arsenal of legends and myths for nation building. And why not aspire to a nation that is free of myths and lies?

I don't know whether or not Jenin constituted a massacre in the legal sense. But does it really matter? What is certain is that homes were destroyed with huge army bulldozers without giving an opportunity for their civilian inhabitants to vacate them and some died under the rubble. This has been confirmed by several witnesses who survived.

One man heard the bulldozer approaching. He went out with his family and began to wave at the driver. He cried after him to stop. He said, 'My father is inside. Wait. Stop. Don't demolish my house.' But the driver did not want to listen. He backed up and came back again, taking a second blow with the mouth of his big machine at the man's house with the father inside. The family now had to make that fateful choice: should they linger and endanger the whole family or should they escape and leave the old man to his death? As they left, they saw their house turn into rubble. No man should be able to impose such a choice on another. This to me is enough of an indictment.

Ali, a professor from Birzeit, was in Jenin and described to me how the camp looks now: 'The Jenin camp is situated on a hill. You walk between houses that have been ruined with only some walls still standing. You walk on through the narrow lanes until you suddenly come upon a flat open space. It is worse than a disaster area which had been struck by an earthquake. This is a man-made disaster. Houses have been demolished by enormous army bulldozers. Then the ground was flattened. It is now a raised platform containing the ruins of people's homes. People who have lost everything would stand with you over the rubble and tell you, "Here, below this spot, stood my house."'

Describing his feelings while the camp was still under siege, one resident said, 'The frustration of seeing around you those in need of help and you are unable to give it. There is nothing you can do for the sick, for those under the rubble, for the orphans. All you have is the hope. The world has heard of Jenin. They followed what happened here day by day. The world expressed outrage. The world will act. There will surely be massive demonstrations that would embarrass Arab regimes to such an extent that they no longer can remain silent. It was Tuesday. We waited until Wednesday and when nothing happened we thought it would happen the next day. When Thursday came and still nothing happened we said, of course, Friday is the day of prayer. It would be the big day for demonstrations. The masses did not want to rise because they were waiting for the big day, Friday. Then it will happen. Friday came and went, and Saturday and Sunday. The days rolled on and there was silence. We lived in the dark, isolated and tired along with our wounded, orphans, destitute and homeless. We waited in vain.'

* * *

During the last lifting of curfew I saw one of the more rumbustious shopkeepers sitting on a low wicker chair next to his shop in the sun. Three tanks were parked opposite his shop on the street. Around them were a number of heavily armed young Israeli soldiers. The old Palestinian shopkeeper, wrapped in an ancient cardigan knitted by his wife, sat sunning himself, seemingly oblivious of their presence.

Our shopkeepers have all spent long days sitting by their shops as the world around them changed. A few have been there since the British mandate times. The slightly younger ones began when the Jordanians ruled this area. Then Israel imposed military rule. They endured this too and survived. When they were ordered to open their shops they complied. Close they closed. They did business when it was possible and sat on their low chairs in the sun when it was slow. They have adopted their own unmistakable way of standing by the door of their business with part of their body inside the shop and part on the pavement, slightly leaning their weight on one leg, feigning relaxation yet anxious and expectant, taking fleeting looks at the action on the street, prepared for any contingency. Attentive always to their work and prepared at the slightest indication of interest by any of the passers-by to put all their weight on the part of their body inside the shop and concentrate fully on their role as merchants.

Those among their rank who could not passively endure this torturous ebb and flow of oppressive measures joined the resistance. Those who remained faithful to their trade would bring their chairs together next to their shops and proceed to discuss the life of the errant merchant and exchange his news among themselves. They always had their own opinion on everything, much like the members of the chorus in Greek tragedies.

The majority of the Palestinian community in the occupied territories are like these men, members in the chorus of this unending tragedy. We all continue to attempt, despite mounting obstacles, to go on with our life. We all have opinions which we express. When we can, we all continue to sun ourselves in direct view of the Israeli tanks and soldiers, as if they were not there. This is how we have been able to survive throughout these past thirty-five years. What these soldiers destroy we repair. When they close roads we find detours. We're always trying to find alternatives for what they deny us.

* * *

The pattern has been set: every few days we are allowed out to inspect what damage has been done since the last time the curfew was lifted. Then the Israeli soldiers begin to shoot again, indicating that our time is over, we must return home and close the door. We are kept shut in for another four or five days, not allowed out for a single moment. Yesterday I was wondering why there was tension in the air and cars being driven recklessly. Then I discovered that a boy of fourteen was killed by the army as he used his 'privilege' of going out for a few hours after being locked in for four days. As we sit at home we hear the sound outside of the destruction caused by the soldiers, who now roam about our streets, driving their tanks through our narrow alleys, going about their business of blasting locks to offices and buildings and wreaking havoc to their insides, going into people's homes and searching, damaging property and arresting the young. When the soldiers get tired or feel they need to shower or to rest, they choose a house, usually the top floor in an apartment building that appears comfortable or which they are perhaps curious to see from the inside. I know many people who have lost all their water to the soldiers. The soldiers walk through the garden (most ground-floor apartments have gardens). With the humid nights and sunny days during this spring, the roses are in full bloom. The geraniums are also covered with gorgeous colour. Into this colourful garden the soldiers tromp. They bang at the door. Point their guns at the inhabitants. Others go up the stairs and bring the families living on upper floors down. Everyone is forced into one apartment, sometimes into one single room in one apartment. They are locked in and the soldiers keep the key. One family who had been locked in during the early days of the occupation for all of the five days until curfew was lifted could not be let out without breaking the door, the soldiers had lost the key. The soldiers now become the new owners. They help themselves to the drinks in the fridge and, contrary to their strict orders, sometimes also to food especially if it is a tempting cake covered with cream, as happened in one house which was celebrating the birthday of a son when the soldiers entered. They use the water to take showers and help themselves to clean towels. After they have cleaned themselves, satiated their thirst with drink, they test which are the best beds and take a nap. Sometimes they spend an afternoon. They have also been known to stay the night. Some of the high apartments they have occupied have a good view of Ramallah. If they looked they would see how hilly and attractive is the town. In most residential areas the streets are lined with trees. At this time the trees are beginning to have new leaves and the jacarandas their beautiful flame flowers. The town has magnificent views and its air is fresh and clean. But the beauty, the quiet pastoral nature of the town, its humanity, do not seem to have touched these soldiers or made them ashamed of acting with such brutality. Next morning, when they're done, they send someone to open the door, if they can remember where they kept the key, and leave the building and proceed on to fulfil other military objectives.

21 April

Last night the Israeli army withdrew from most of Ramallah. Salwa left her house early after she heard the army vacated her office, which is across the street from her house. She found that the entire metal front door had been removed. She had been expecting a mess but was not prepared for what she saw. Everything had been removed and thrown into one room. Her computers, photocopier, all the machinery had been wrecked and her hard disks had been systematically removed. As she was rummaging through the piles of refuse left by the army, three men appeared. Salwa's father was an Anglican priest. She grew up on the stories from the Bible. These men must have reminded her of Lazarus, because they looked as though they had arisen from the dead. They had long beards. They looked gaunt and pale. They frightened her.

'What do you want?' she asked.

'Nothing. We've just come to look at what the army did here.'

'Where are you from?' she asked them.

'We have been hiding across the street in the garage right there. We had very little food. Mainly dry chickpeas, which we soaked in water and ate. When the curfew was lifted the soldiers did not leave this post and so we couldn't move out.'

They looked around at the damage in silence and left.

* * *

Like many others I have spent all day going on inspection tours to witness the destruction wrought by the Israeli army to homes and institutions around Ramallah. I was expecting to see terrible devastation. I had read over the Internet in the Israeli newspaper *Ha'aretz* that the IDF admitted what was described as 'ugly vandalism' against Palestinian property. An army source was quoted as saying, 'It was not an order from above but that's how it was understood in the field. The infantry, both the conscripts and the reservists who accompanied the intelligence teams, understood that they were allowed – or indeed expected – to destroy the property in the offices.'

There was a consistent pattern to the vandalism that I saw: data was destroyed, whether it was an optician's, dental or medical clinic or the Ministry of Education. The army had destroyed it either by wrecking the machines in which it was saved, throwing around the files or removing the hard disk and taking it along with them. In those ministries like the Ministry of Culture where the army spent a number of days, the destruction was total. Nothing had been left unbroken. In other ministries, such as Public Works, the office was dynamited. In one American–Canadian franchise restaurant everything was destroyed. Every single lamp in the ceiling was shot. The messages the soldiers wrote on the walls were in English and were mainly taken from American soldiers' idiom, such as 'Born to Kill' and 'Eat, Drink and Destroy', which sometimes was varied to, 'Eat, Drink and Shit.' Other messages were home-grown: 'Fucking Arabs Never Mess with Us Again.' At the Ministry of Culture, where the damage was systematic and nothing was kept intact, the final image painted on the door, which one saw upon leaving the building, was the menorah with the word 'Israel' written underneath.

April 22

Leaving or entering Ramallah has remained difficult, even after the army has withdrawn from the town for we continue to be under siege. Our friend Suad had to travel to Amman to visit her mother. After walking across the new border, she found a taxi to take her through dirt roads that avoided the Israeli blockade. The car was bumping over stones and falling into holes on narrow paths along the hills until it got to the point where it could go no further. They found themselves down in the wadi with no way of going any further. The only possible path was just too steep for the car to climb. The driver made several attempts to force his car to move, to no avail. Suad thought her journey was going to end there when she saw a tractor coming down the hill. They attached the car to it and were pulled up the steep hill. And so the journey proceeded. It was only her resourcefulness and sense of humor that sustained her throughout this ordeal. At lunch time she made her companions stop and picnic in the lee of a large rock in the countryside she loves and which had long been out of bounds for her. The journey that usually takes one hour took eight.

There must be thousands of workers in nearby villages who depend on Ramallah for work of which they have been deprived throughout this month. Today Majdi, a man in his mid-thirties, came to my house seeking work. He lives in Jiljiliah, a village north of Ramallah, with his family of five. I noticed that he was limping. I asked him what happened.

'Our life is bitter,' he began by saying, with a look of revulsion sweeping over his open face. 'One has no spirit any longer, no will to live. They are doing whatever they can to make it hard on us. Last week I decided to look for work. I went with my brother-in-law to East Jerusalem. We were able to find work for the day. We were returning home in the afternoon when an Israeli jeep stopped us. They asked to see our work permits. We didn't have them. "Get into the jeep," they said. I heard them call their head-quarters to check on us. They were told that our record was *nake* [clean]. I can understand Hebrew. I heard their commander tell them to drop us at the checkpoint and let us go. They didn't. They drove us through a field and, when they reached a deserted house, they stopped, took us down and began to beat us up. I told them, "I don't care. Kill me if you like." I felt prepared to die. What use is this life? They hit me with their gun and, when I was on the ground, kicked me with their boots until I was all bruised and bleeding. Then they left us and drove off. It took us over an hour to get to the main road and find a taxi to take us back home.'

I saw two pictures in the local paper which I thought said it all. The first was of a Palestinian man, tall with bent head, walking pensively along with his scarfed wife and children by a tank. The caption said that he was returning home after the curfew was imposed. The other was of a man loading a water jug and shopping bags on a donkey going up on an unpaved small hill because the Israeli army had blocked the road leading to his house and he could not use a car to get to it.

How different are these pictures from those of the victorious young men with guns or stones shooting or throwing stones at the Israeli army.

A woman friend of mine whose husband works with

UNRWA was able to use her UN car to travel on the main road from Jerusalem to Nablus. She described what she saw on the road: 'All I could see on the way were Israeli cars. Whenever there was a car with a West Bank license plate it had been driven off the road. The army would stop its driver, order him to hand over the key and leave him stranded. Hebrew road signs for the settlements were all over. It was like being in Israel.'

No wonder the settlers now driving in the West Bank can honestly report that they see only Jews when they travel between the settlements that dot the hills, for only Jews are allowed on the roads. Israeli schools and colleges have opened campuses in some of these settlements and large industrial zones have been established, employing thousands of workers. Some settlements have grown to be the size of cities. The doggedness of successive Israeli governments in pursuit of the policy of settlements has come to fruition. The entire area of geographic Palestine is now settled by Israeli Jews. A road network has been developed to connect them to each other and to Israel, bypassing, sometimes through tunnels, the eight isolated Palestinian enclaves. The need to protect existing settlements and to plan new ones is a key element in the policy of Ariel Sharon's government. He has declared that he wants to attract a million Jews to Greater Israel.

When the early Jewish settlers first came to Palestine it was predominantly inhabited by Arabs. They had a vision which coloured how they saw the land. They persisted against all odds until everyone else could see what they saw without their trained ideological eyes. I'm told that even now the expansion of settlements around Ramallah is continuing apace. Givat Ze'ev, the settlement to the south-west, has been expanded over a number of hills to the west and down into the valley. And so has

Psagot to the east and Dolev to the north. More roads and bridges and tunnels have been built. The Modi'in bloc of settlements, straddling the 1967 border between Israel and the West Bank, includes full-fledged cities. The process that began in earnest in 1968 has continued without interruption ever since. In every aspect of our life, we the Palestinians are paying a heavy price for this policy. Israeli security forces monitor our isolated enclaves thus enabling settlers to pursue a 'normal' life. Settlements, not Palestinian towns, enjoy uninterrupted continuity. Palestinians, not settlers, bear the primary burden created by security arrangements for the latter.

Confined as we are to the small enclave of Ramallah, we try to make the most of what we've got. Today Penny and I went shopping for almonds and cashews from Audeh's nut shop on the other side of town. To get there we had to avoid the leadership compound. Irsal Street, which we needed to cross, remains blocked with huge piles of rubble and pieces of metal. We had to find another way.

'Let's go the long way,' Penny said.

We did. We drove around the hills below the Muqata to the Snobar swimming pool, owned by our old neighbour, Amin, who has been unable to open it this summer, and the YWCA, which also could not open.

'Shall I put on music?' Penny asked. 'We can pretend we are on an excursion.'

The Brahms sonata filled the car as we drove as slowly as we could to prolong the drive along the edge of town, by the side of the hill, looking at the wadi where there are clusters of pine trees and olives and empty hills and an unimpeded view of the horizon.

25 April

There are many meetings and day conferences being held to discuss the general political situation. I have just been to one at the house of my neighbour Sami. The meeting was dominated by Nadeem, a veteran politician who has been with Fatah throughout his political life. He was also a member of Arafat's government. He began by giving an example of how Arafat works. He said that after he became a minister, a woman came to him seeking his help. She had obtained funds for a test-tube baby twice but both attempts had failed. She wanted the *sulta*'s (Palestinian Authority) support for a third attempt. Nadeem knew that there was a rule for subsidizing only two attempts. But he thought he would try. So he went to Arafat, who wrote that she should be paid for further attempts until she gets pregnant, 'God permitting'.

Nadeem was critical of Arafat for getting involved in every detail. He said he was sure that upon his release from the Muqata, Arafat would spend a month going around getting cheered for his victory in surviving. But ultimately, Nadeem thought, people will blame the *sulta* for what happened. The government must resign and a new, better-run government must be appointed.

There were others in that meeting who did not think this was enough. To them it was too little too late.

27 April

Around eight in the morning I went to the nearby plant nursery to get some summer seedlings. It is situated on the slope of one of the eastern hills. As I was leaving, I heard gunshots coming from the north-east.

Abu Zaki, who was helping me take the plants to my car, stopped. 'The firing is coming from the direction of Surda, on the way to Birzeit University,' he said. Then he added in a low monotone, 'The soldiers are shooting to make them flee. They're also throwing tear gas.'

After dropping the plants in the boot of the car, I stood alone, looking at the smoking horizon, thinking of the students and faculty trying to get to their university at eight o'clock in the morning and what they have to put up with, of bullets and tear gas on a beautiful clear morning at the end of April.

In the afternoon I took my nephew and niece to buy them presents in celebration of the end of the curfew. Aziz will soon be celebrating his seventh birthday. I was only nine years older when the occupation began and I've had to endure it ever since. I hope it will turn out differently for him.

We parked the car in the car park next to the Midan Building. I noticed that the children did not look up at the burnt building. They made no comments and asked no questions. We crossed the car park and climbed up the stairs to Main Street to the toy shop. Tala bought accessories for her doll. Aziz was not sure what he wanted. His attention was drawn to a tank. At first he seemed interested in buying it. But after he gave it a quick examination, he quickly decided against it. He had seen the real thing and this was too flimsy to use as an object of his fantasies.

Before returning home, I went to visit the Muqata. I had to climb a high mound of rubble placed at the main entrance, which was the only way to get into the compound during the Israeli occupation. I used to come here often when I represented clients at the military court. My last visit was in 1995, when the Israeli army withdrew from Ramallah.

This place has always evoked strong emotions in me. I walked around the wreckage and rubble and found that, contrary to what I had expected, the army had not demolished the old Tegart Building but had only gutted its walls. I was distressed to find out that the Palestinian Authority had left the military court in the same place where it had been during the time of Israeli rule. A sign in Arabic announced, 'Mahkameh askaria'. The prison was also still there, but not the high gate before which I had so often stood as I rang the bell for the guard to open it so that I could visit a client. Next to the prison the PA had built an annexe that was connected by an overpass to the old cement structure. The new white-stone building had a large glass door embossed with the PA insignia of the eagle. Inside were the fancy halls for the reception of diplomats. Rather than make a break with the past, demolish or turn this hated Tegart into a museum, an annexe was built to accommodate the activities of the new regime. Inside this compound were no less than fifty cars, smashed and strewn all over the grounds. The compound that had become the symbol of a Palestinian victory after the Israeli army evacuated it has now been turned into a sad monument of yet another Palestinian defeat.

When I got home I had to change all my clothes and take a shower. I was covered in dust.

* * *

The various entrances to Ramallah remain blocked, with no vehicular movement allowed. Often at night I hear shooting and I am told the army is on an excursion into the town. The night also brings the sound of barking dogs, as though one were sleeping in the wild. Without municipal services to manage the dogs that invade from the hills to scavenge the piling garbage in the streets, they and the Israeli soldiers take over our town after dark. Who would dare go out at night? It would be death by shooting or attack from possibly rabid dogs.

28 April

I went to visit my dentist. I could hardly recognize the clinic. In the course of exploding open a door opposite, the army had caused the entire wall of his clinic to collapse. His sterilization machine was destroyed. He said he needed a week to get a new machine and clean up. I shall have to endure my toothache for another week.

After leaving the ruined clinic I walked through the Manara roundabout, examining the plastic lion without the tail. At the beginning of Main Street, on the wall of the carpet shop, I saw newly posted pictures of *shuhada*. I stopped to look. The men featured there did not look typical. They had no defiant look or a display of firearms. They didn't stand with the picture of the Dome of the Rock in the background. The pictures used looked like passport photographs. They were of older, middle-aged, spectacled men unlikely to be candidates for martyrdom. I read the caption on the poster. It described them as the martyrs killed in the battle for the Arizona Building defending the FIDA office. It doesn't take a Muslim theologian to know that there needs to be an element of volition for the attainment of the status of a *shaheed*. Those responsible for placing these men in a life-threatening situation and abandoning them to their fate cannot be exonerated simply by describing the senseless death of these guards in these lofty religious terms. How much has this society suffered for the irresponsibility of its leaders?

Further down Main Street I found the barber shop open. All that my barber needs to function are scissors and his dextrous hands. Fortunately he hasn't lost these. I went in and waited for my turn. It was a long wait, because so many others also have not had a haircut for over a month. When my turn came, the barber wanted to tell me all about his experience during the occupation. What I heard from him confirmed what I had been suspecting, that the battle of Ramallah was a mock battle. Like a Don Quixote, the Israeli army, operating battle tanks around the house of my mother and her neighbours, was fighting its own shadow in a battle that it can never win.

My barber was well positioned to have a good view of the action, because he lives in the centre of town, on the ground floor of the Chamber of Commerce Building. His main door opens to the car park where the tanks that shelled the Midan Building were stationed.

'Can you imagine being next to these huge machines, firing their big guns?' he told me. 'I tell you, it was hell. I lived through hell. When the firing started, I felt the whole house was going to crumble. Then it stopped and I heard the soldiers screaming, "We will count until ten. If you are not out we will blow up the building." They began: "One, two, three ..." and I was left wondering, Do they mean us? Should we get out or stay? Finally we decided to go out. My mother went first. She held up a white sheet. I walked behind her. When the soldiers saw us, they shouted, "Go back in. Go back."

'But the blasting didn't stop even after everyone in the Midan Building had left. The first four days were the worst, but it didn't stop afterwards. I watched them. They would move their tanks one way and then drive down Post Office Street and begin

133

shelling, then they would turn around, go up, take another position, as though they were in a battle field, and, I promise you, there was no one returning fire. We would first hear a whiz, then *Boom* as the shell hit. They didn't only aim at the Midan Building, they also hit the Housing Bank, the shoe shop, the Chamber of Commerce and the PFLP office, all of them around where I live. We heard every one of these blasts. Every single one. No other household lived the hell we endured. I have youngsters in the house and they were so scared. One of them was sick. But I couldn't get out and bring him a doctor. How could I? I needed medicine but forget it. I couldn't get medicine. We spent a hell of a time in our house, I tell you. A hell of a time.

'At the end of many terrible ordeals, they entered my house to search it. Then began another ordeal. Before they left, I got my chance. I don't know how I got the words to say all these things. It was as though the frustration of weeks had given me inspiration and eloquence that I could make a stone shed tears. I told this soldier, "Let's forget about everything, about the war, about the land, about Hamas, about everything. This is a case of human beings. Do you consider me a human being? If not, then I will crawl on all fours and lick your boots. But if you do, then you must realize that I also have rights. You have violated all these rights. You came in. You terrorized my family. You left us without food and medicine. My youngest was sick and I couldn't get him medicine. You used your weapons and burnt the building on top and I had to endure two days of fumes. Then you bombarded this building next to me for days and I endured. Then, after all this, you come into my house. You respect nothing of my life. You search the underwear of my dead wife. You take my private pictures. You even consider a piece of embroidery on the door which says 'Peace and Justice for Palestine' as posing a danger to you. You throw it on the ground and you stamp on it. You terrorize my son. You take him over and try and cajole him and ask him to tell you about his father, as though his father was a criminal. You take the shell of a bullet from your own gun and you want to find out from him: does your father have a gun, does he tell you to do things? I could see how my son turned all white with fright. You pretend to care and ask me to bring him water. Now you have the gun and feel you have the power to act in this way. One day someone will come with greater power than you and will do the same to you. We can't go on like this. We have to learn to respect each other."

'The soldier finally began to listen. He seemed sorry and apologetic. Had these soldiers left without giving me this opportunity to release what I felt in my heart, I don't know what would have happened to me. I would have burst. Now I felt better. Vindicated. The soldier listened. I believe I may have made him think, even change his mind about us Palestinians. I told Kareem, "Son, go make me a large whisky." It was three in the morning, but I now thought a whisky would be the right way to end this.'

I thought that my barber had now finished and would get on with the haircut. But he still had more to say. He stepped back, holding the comb and looking at his face in the mirror.

'I forgot to tell you,' he said. 'At one point, after they had bombarded the hell out of the building, one soldier took a mannequin from one of the shops and proceeded to fuck it in the middle of the car park. Then another came and wanted his turn. He pulled at the arm and it broke. So he went back into the shop and got a new one. He brought it to the middle of the car park and the other soldiers came and they all joined in an orgy of fucking dummies in my front yard.'

I might have stayed all afternoon listening to the experiences of the other customers during this latest Israeli occupation. Everyone had a story to tell. But one Shylock speech delivered in Ramallah by a Palestinian to a Jew was enough for me. I had work to do at the office.

When I stepped out of the shop I could see across the street the depressing sight of the Arizona Building with its two top floors gutted and burned. In a sort of a purification ritual, shop-keepers with brooms were obsessively cleaning the pavements, the theatre of the action in the tragedy in which they play the chorus. Walking back to the office, I met with armed young men, some in uniform, others in civilian clothes. They had come out of hiding and dug out their guns from beneath the farm wall. The shop-owners on Main Street sat on low chairs sunning themselves. And everything seemed back to the way it has always been.

∗ ∗ ∗

The banner across the Main Street announcing a new art exhibition at the municipality hall said, 'Like a phoenix we shall arise from the ashes. The best days are yet to come.' In the afternoon Penny and I went to visit the exhibition.

It was housed in an unfinished basement below the municipality. It has been decades since this building was erected. The town expanded and grew but the council responsible for its administration has remained frozen in time. The last elections took place in 1976. The Palestinian Authority followed the practice established by the Israeli military of appointing the council rather than allowing elections to be conducted.

In this cavernous hall the designers of the exhibition used several ordering principles, including grouping objects by type and setting, from domestic furnishings to office equipment to bathrooms. Two rows of broken computer screens were arranged through the centre of the room. A television smashed by a sharp object was placed next to a reading chair at a drunken tilt, with a broken remote control on the ground nearby. A plant was placed in an empty filing cabinet. Penny called it in a review she wrote, 'Ramallah Dada'.

The artists who organized the exhibition used texts which, Penny wrote, 'are sometimes used to contrast the ordinary with the absurd, but more often to carry the spectator to another realm – a realm of dreams and of the future'. An eye is painted on one broken computer and a line of text reads, 'The path is an open eye to see things.' The message on a dangling door reads, 'The broken door is a wide space.' Nearby was a dry fishbowl containing an empty sardine can. The inscription reads, 'Don't forget to feed the fish.' But this last inscription was not written for the exhibition. An Israeli soldier who had occupied a Ramallah residence left this message behind after he dumped the water out of the fishbowl and dangled the sardine can from his army ration.

On one side of the room was a large screen on which a video machine projected images of Ramallah's damaged streets and institutions. I strolled through these different exhibits until I got to the last wall, on which was placed a giant photo-collage showing damage to various homes and institutions. I stood before these images and began to scrutinize them. I had visited many houses and institutions and felt the rage against the perpetrators of this destruction. Now that I was before a photographic representation, I had enough distance to allow other emotions to be felt. This time I found myself thinking about the soldiers who were responsible for this. In a recent article in the Israeli press, a sex worker in Tel Aviv was quoted as saying, 'Since Operation Defensive Shield began, there's been an increase in the number of men asking for sado-masochism. Among them are some who never tried it before and perhaps never would have if they lived a more balanced and stable life. I understand it as a counter-reaction to the constant need to be the strong one, the occupier and the decider.'

The indiscriminate destruction captured by the pictures on the wall was not done in the heat of battle when the soldiers were in danger for their life, rather in a deliberate, wilful, premeditated fashion. Young men with guns or other implements of destruction walked into people's homes and institutions in broad daylight, breaking, smashing and destroying computer screens, televisions, medical and sound equipment, furniture, toilets, wall hangings, children's toys – whatever they found. What could they have been told about us that made them so full of rage and hatred that they were able to perpetrate these raving raids without protest? They must have fathers and mothers, brothers and sisters, wives and perhaps children of their own. How could they go back to them after this?

For the first time throughout this long month I found myself thinking about these soldiers not as intimidating objects of destruction but as human beings. And for the first time I found myself feeling compassion for them, for their relatives and the society they have to go back to, which, after all, will always be a neighbour of ours. This new emotion filled me with a profound sense of relief. For the first time during this long month I was able to overcome the crippling anger that had gripped me throughout this invasion.

I left the exhibition thinking how compassion in this part of the world was in short supply, compassion for ourselves and what has become of our life, and compassion for our enemies. After all, we are both in the same sinking boat.

EPILOGUE

18 November

Today was our fourteenth wedding anniversary. The first Intifada was a year old when we got married in Jerusalem. On the way to my wedding I saw a soldier slap a young man as we passed Amari Refugee Camp. I wanted to stop. I was still active in human rights. But my brother, who was the best man, drove on. He didn't want me to be late for my wedding.

We had what we called an Intifada wedding. This meant a simple ceremony. We didn't print wedding invitations. We announced the occasion by word of mouth and a notice at Al Haq's bulletin board. A few days before our big event, the PLO in Tunis declared the establishment of a Palestinian state. The Israeli military imposed a curfew and cut off our electricity. Penny's parents had come from Illinois for the wedding. We had to entertain them with a game of Scrabble played in candlelight.

The exceptional times relieved us of many of the conventional demands associated with weddings here. Those who cared to be with us on our happy day found a way to bypass the checkpoint and get to Saint George's Cathedral in Jerusalem where the wedding was celebrated. Afterwards we had an intimate party in the cathedral courtyard under the arcades. We didn't travel to a romantic location for our honeymoon. We drove back to our home in Ramallah where the Intifada was raging. But we didn't feel deprived. We were part of a social and political transformation that would not only bring about the end of the Israeli occupation but also the creation of a new society more egalitarian, humane and democratic.

Contrary to our initial expectations, the Intifada dragged on for years. Our days were full of different sorts of confrontations with the Israeli army and so were our nights. We spent many sleepless nights expecting the army to knock at our door and force us down to paint over graffiti or remove a stone blockade placed by young activists. It was not only the harassment, those were dangerous times.

Two years after we got married I came close to losing Penny. She heard loud sounds and went to our glass veranda to look out. A group of passing settlers raised their machine gun and sprayed the window. Fortunately, their aim was poor. The mounting difficulties and danger only increased our determination to continue with our struggle until the end of the Israeli occupation.

My role in that first Intifada was clear. I was part of the legal struggle. Both through my law practice and at Al Haq we used every legal means available to challenge the Israeli violations of international law. We made constant references to the Hague Regulations and the Fourth Geneva Convention. A case was being built against Israel. We didn't let anything go. Every expropriation of land, every land use and road scheme was challenged. We had backers and allies throughout the world. The support for Palestinian rights and the conviction that Israeli settlements were illegal extended to a significant sector of Israeli society who joined in many common actions against these illegalities. A clear communicable legal narrative was being developed which was helping remove some of the deliberate obfuscation which Israel was doing its best to propagate.

Then on 13 September 1991, four years after the start of the Intifada, the negotiations began between Israel and the joint Jordanian Palestinian Delegation. We were thrilled. We always knew the resistance was a means, not an end. The end would be a political compromise and this could only come through negotiations. Both Penny and I were involved in the Washington talks, assisting the Palestinian Delegation; I as a legal advisor, Penny as a staff writer and human rights resource person.

Two years later, after secret negotiations in Oslo, an agreement was reached between Israel and the PLO on a Declaration of Principles. The Occupied Territories were divided into three areas with Israel retaining full control over the settlements. There was no insistence on a settlement freeze which the Delegation in Washington had made a condition for entering into any agreement with Israel. The PLO must have calculated that by accepting Oslo it would gain a respite from the pressure it was facing. What it failed to realize was that the very design of Oslo would prevent it from using the interim period to improve its situation for the final status talks. Quite the contrary. As the negotiations were proceeding for a final agreement more settlements were being built and existing ones expanded at a faster pace than ever, doubling the number of settlers in the West Bank. It took several years before people were able to grasp the disaster that was the Oslo Accords. When they did, the second Intifada broke out. How different is my response to the present struggle from what it was then.

A few weeks ago when the curfew was still in force, I was staying up late working. It was already midnight when I heard the announcement by a young man using his strong voice to bid all of us, the inhabitants of the Tireh neighborhood where I live, to leave our houses and assemble at the Manarah roundabout in the centre of town where a demonstration in defiance of the curfew would begin. 'Enough submission,' he declared, 'President Arafat is in danger. Not only is he threatened, the whole nation is. I urge everyone, young and old, women and men, leave your houses now and join the peaceful demonstration. Enough submission, enough, enough.'

Hearing this call brought back memories of the first Intifada which had continued for seven long and difficult years. The caller began with the word '*Nida*', [call] which he repeated three times. This was how all the communiqués of the first Intifada opened. The sound of the caller was getting louder. He was approaching my house. But I don't want to be stirred again to repeat a struggle under a leadership which has brought me only despair. I want to be left alone. I found myself turning off all the lights, closing all the windows and going to bed.

Next day I learned that thousands had heeded the call, women and men, young and old. Late into the night, the streets were full of unarmed civilians some marching in defiance of the curfew, others standing at their front yards beating pots and pans. Chants could be heard from across the hills as the crowd was joined by others from nearby villages, carrying the Palestinian flag and climbing over the blockades to march to the center of Ramallah chanting, 'Israelis Go Home'. What a simple formula for peace: Israelis go home and leave us to live our life in Palestine!

From my experience of the first Intifada I know how formidable unarmed civilians can be when they are determined to resist. But the struggle is only the means, not the end. I had been through the bitter experience of witnessing the leadership undermine the legal struggle which I worked so hard to develop.

143

I had no faith that this impenitent leadership would do any better now.

✳ ✳ ✳

This morning I was awakened before daybreak by an Israeli soldier announcing curfew:

'To the inhabitants of Ramallah, curfew is imposed by order of the military governor. Whoever violates this order will be punished.'

The caller repeated this announcement over and over as a reminder to us that the army of occupation is still here, is still victorious and can make orders which everyone must obey. Half asleep I mumbled, 'OK I got the message, now go away and let me sleep'. But he persisted.

Awakened, I was plagued with the inevitable series of ruminations and worries. Have they gone to Samer's house again? Will they take it over as they did the last time? It's good we shopped. Does mother have her prescription drugs? Penny would be unable to travel to the States now to visit her parents. The review of my affairs and concerns over, I went back to sleep after closing the window.

At six however the curfew call woke me up again. I made coffee and Penny opened her eyes – coffee was more effective than curfew announcements. When I told her the news she thought I was joking. Then the caller came again and immediately the telephone began to ring. I thought it must be my mother (whom we have started calling *Khabar Ajel* [breaking news] because she calls immediately after any new happening). But it wasn't. It was Rita.

'They are searching your area', Rita said in her breathless voice. 'They have just been to Shamieh's and they are coming to your house.' She sounded as though she could see the movements of the army on a screen before her.

I put down the receiver and yelled the news to Penny who was still in bed. I had not showered or shaved yet. I was still in my dressing gown. Should I meet them like this? No. I better be dressed. I went quickly to the dressing room when the doorbell began ringing. Fortunately, we don't have the old fashioned bell which you can hold for a continuous persistent, annoying sound. We have installed one that makes three delicate notes with a civilized interval between each of them. Then it rests. If you press it again it would repeat the cycle. But you cannot get it to go faster however hard you press even if you were a soldier in the Israeli army.

I heard Penny bravely call out: 'I'll get it.'

I stood before my clothes: what's the best thing to wear, casual or formal? I decided on casual. I picked up my sand-coloured corduroys and the striped green and grey shirt. I put on my shoes (I did not want to be in thongs even though they gave me extra height) and rushed. They were already in the house, six of them. Their commander was small with a stubble for a beard. He did not look vicious. One of them was blond and Russian looking. He said 'Shalom' and I returned the greeting.

'Do you speak Hebrew,' he asked.

'A little,' I said. But then we continued in English.

'We want to look around,' he said.

'You know you need a warrant. Do you have one?'

'No,' he said, with a snigger. 'We are not police. We are the army.'

145

'Yes,' I said, 'I can see this. But even the army needs a warrant.'

'No,' he said.

I said: 'I know. I am a lawyer.'

But he just proceeded into my house with his elaborate uniform and machine gun. The house is built around an inner courtyard. Three soldiers went left and three took to the right walking towards me. Penny watched the first three, while I followed the others. The commander approached me. He was my height. He pulled a picture from one of his many pockets. It was a studio picture of a young man taken against a dreamy vista of greenery with a lake.

'We're looking for this man,' he said. 'Do you know him?'

'No I don't,' I said trying to keep my eyes on the soldier going into my living room and the one going into the kitchen. He looked at the garage door to the left, where I keep my diaries.

'This leads to the outside?' he asked in Hebrew, then repeated the question in English.

I said yes. He didn't want me to open it instead he went into the pantry then out again. I lost track of the third soldier who had already disappeared into our bedroom. When he left it he came face to face with his armed colleagues accompanied by Penny who were making their round from the other side. Startled he lifted his gun, his finger on the trigger ready to shoot. He only stopped when he realized who they were.

Now the search was over. But the soldiers still lingered. I saw one of them take out his water bottle from a side pocket. He tried to drink but it was empty. I felt he was indicating to me that he wanted to fill it up. Instinctively I was going to offer him water but then remembered Abu Issa who told his wife to make tea for the soldiers who came to arrest his son. 'Are you crazy?' his wife screamed. No I wasn't going to be a sop like Abu Issa. I resisted the temptation to be civil to a soldier coming to search my house.

The commander now asked to see my identity card. As he examined it I looked more closely at his face. He was young, not older than early twenties. How malleable people are at this age. Now I could understand the despairing rage of my Israeli friends with young sons. The army claims their children when they are still at an impressionable age. These youngsters could not have made up their own minds. They are instruments in the hands of the older men in power in Israel.

As the commander of this unit was taking down the details from my identity card I looked at the others. One of them was fiddling with his pockets. Their uniform had so many pockets. Each seemed to have something. From one he pulled a straw and began sucking at it. Did he have a container of soft drink hidden there. I couldn't tell. Another asked his colleague for help to take something bluish out of another pocket which he could not reach while holding his machine gun. They were like kids distracted by their drinks, sharing the water bottle, digging their hands into deep pouches all around their waists and down each leg, where they seemed to keep little treats tucked inside, along with the odd grenade. Were they able to see me as I could see them? Were they aware of Penny and me as fellow human beings? But none of them met our gaze.

Then their commander lifted his head and asked me: 'Are you from Gaza?'

'No,' I said. It took me a minute to realize that he was wondering if I was related to an Islamic Jihad militant who was assassinated along with his family and neighbors.

I was relieved when they left our house and heard their jeep drive away. I rushed and closed the gate and locked our metal door.

In the evening the curfew was lifted and Samer was able to visit. He had spoken to some of the people whose homes were searched. The soldiers had not always been so well-behaved. They had caused a lot of damage and left huge messes behind them. Perhaps by noontime they were frustrated from repeating the same thing over and over and failing to find the man they wanted. I tried to think: who among those young men was the villain? Or were they all?

* * *

Last April I spent many nights living in fear of the army breaking into my house. Now that it had happened it was an anticlimax just like the period we are living through now. I had wanted to think of the events of last April as representing a climax that would be followed by a strong reaction, a resolution, an end. But it was not to be. There was no outcry, not from the Israeli public, not from the world. No one came to our assistance. The invading army carried out its wild acts of wanton destruction and murder and withdrew to the peripheries retaining their siege on our town and our life. Those harrowing times were followed by months of a twenty-four-hour curfew that the army lifted only for a few hours every two or three days. For months Ramallah, along with most other towns and villages in the West Bank, remained in a state of involuntary dormancy, its workers not allowed to work, its students struggling to get to their schools and universities, its economic life brought to a halt.

The West Bank had been turned into the biggest detention camp in the world.

My other fear has been of the Israeli army expelling us *en masse* from the Occupied Territories. This fear seems to have been unfounded. Israel might have realized that it would not be able to get away with an ethnic cleansing of this sort. So it is using a different tactic. Even when the Chief of Staff acknowledges an area is quiet, he still keeps it under curfew. Curfew is an extraordinary measure. It is usually imposed during a state of emergency, for a short period of time, when the authority in power is unable to restore public order. When it is inflicted on a civilian population for a prolonged, open-ended period, it is meant to serve a wholly different, more pernicious purpose: the slow strangulation of the community.

Under international law the occupier is responsible for the welfare of the local population. But under the Oslo Accords Israel transferred to the Palestinian Authority responsibility over civilian affairs. The April invasion managed to bring an end to all other aspects of the Oslo Accords except for this. By its destruction of the ministries in the April invasion, the present siege of Palestinian communities and prolonged curfews and economic boycotts, the Israeli army is making it very difficult for the Palestinian Authority to fulfill its responsibilities of providing services to the local population. In every way Israel relates to these territories as sovereign, expropriating lands, building and expanding settlements, and encouraging its population to settle, treating the land as part of the rest of Israel. But it assumes no responsibility for the welfare of the local Palestinian community.

As a result people are often unable to get to work, their children cannot get to school, their lives are disrupted by prolonged curfews and restrictions on every aspect of their life. So naturally they begin to seek opportunities outside Palestine and we witness a steady stream of 'voluntary' exiles. The number of my own friends who have left or are thinking of leaving is increasing by the day. Society is losing its best, its most educated and qualified the like of whom it would take years to replace. The April bang has given way to a more insidious steady state that is no less destructive of the fabric of our civil society.

I don't know why it was yesterday that I felt the full horror of our situation. Perhaps because I realized that this would be the third Christmas that we will spend in these terrible conditions, or maybe because I was able to leave Ramallah and see what was taking place in the countryside around us. The settlements are continuing to expand, the roads are open to Israeli cars but every exit to a Palestinian town or village is blocked. As I looked at the Palestinian cars struggling to find passable paths through mud roads between the rocky hills to get from village to village, I remembered the Israeli High Court's response to our challenge to the 1984 road plan which required expropriation of extensive areas of agricultural land from these Palestinian farmers. The roads are for the benefit of the local population, the court had said.

An English friend who works for an international organization was returning at night to Jerusalem from a work visit to Nablus. The road was deserted, he told me. On both sides were large stretches of olive fields which he had enjoyed looking at during his morning drive north to the city. When he got halfway to Jerusalem he saw to his right an entire olive orchard on fire. It was a dark, moonless night. Above he could see the glittering lights of the settlements dominating the hills and down below the unprotected Palestinian orchard, its thousand trees ablaze, beacons of the anger and destructive transformation of this ancient, cursed land. 'It was an awesome sight,' he said. 'These trees were not planted in clusters there was some distance between them. This could not have been a bush fire. It was arson.'

Not only had the settlers prevented the farmers from reaching their orchards to pick the olives during this last olive-picking season, they were now burning these ancient trees. At moments like these, faced with such horror, I am filled with a profound fear.

The strangers have taken root. They have established modern communities that are better planned, funded and organized than ours. They are supported by the power and might of the Israeli state and army. During the few years when the Palestinian Authority had the full unhindered control over civilian matters and access to huge funds from the rich countries of the world, it did little to improve the ability of our communities to withstand the Israeli onslaught.

From past experience I know that political changes, once they occur, will be followed by very quick transformations on all fronts. I do not know whether a change will take place in the foreseeable future and this land will once again become a pleasant, civilized place where all its inhabitants, Palestinians and Israeli Jews, can live in peace. For now we remain resilient carrying on with our life as best we can. Penny is still able to go on with her writing. Samer's insurance business has been severely affected by the general collapse of the economic system but this has turned him into a better father who is able to spend more time with his family.

His children, Tala and Aziz, are doing well. There are no apparent psychological scars from that horrific experience they went through when the soldiers took over their house. Aziz has lost the extra weight he put on during the month of the invasion from compulsive eating and confinement in the house. I had always hoped to get them started with hill-walking at an early age to inculcate in them the love of the outdoor. Aziz is already seven and for the past three years we have not been able to manage any walks in the hills and valleys around our house. When he visits I try to get him interested in carpentry. I thought we would build a playhouse but he wanted to make a sword and this is what we are working on now.

My mother is hoping to live to see the end of this tragic story. In 1948, as a young woman she participated in a demonstration in Haifa. Half a century later she decided to try again. She joined an unusual performance of the annual Christmas concert of the Jerusalem choir, established in 1954, but now unable to perform in Jerusalem. So they went to the Kalandia checkpoint. Among the squalor and confusion of waiting cars and carts transporting bags back and forth and the hordes of people of all ages crossing this new border on foot, the members of the Jerusalem choir, their conductor sitting in a wheelchair, sang their songs of love, peace and joy. My mother stood among them under the rain. She carried a placard which read: End the occupation now. Israelis go home.

Ramallah
20 December 2002